POSSESSIONS? POWER? PLEASURE?

TRAITS

TEMPERAMENTS

LIFE STORY

THE WHO I AM

WORLDVIEW

PENETRATING QUESTIONS

A Template To Becoming Your True Self

ROGER MAHLOCH

Also by Roger Mahloch:
A Dialogue with My Soul

Table of Contents

Acknowledgments

It was my spiritual director for many years Monsignor Chester P. Michael [10/17/1916—7/31/2014], who opened my heart and mind to many of the convictions I hold true today. Monsignor Michael has touched not only my life but thousands of other lives with his wisdom and unconditional love.

I believe that fate has a way to leading me to be in the right place at the right time. The blessing is when I realize the opportunity at hand and take advantage of it. Meeting Susan Weiss, a spiritual friend, has been a blessing to me. We shared suggestions and advice that augmented my decision to write this book.

I read Father Richard Rohr's meditations daily. (Center for Action and Contemplation) - (CAC.org)

I have quoted him often in this book as his daily meditations often touch my heart. His work is quoted to emphasize what I am trying to express to the reader. Father Rohr's gift of expression along with his staff at CAC have led so many closer to God and to seek their true self. His meditations and books were an inspiration for me to write this book, sharing the template I use to becoming the real me.

I am thankful to Elias Awad for hours sharing his knowledge and thoughts. He directed me to subjects and organization with insight and comments, ones I may not have considered without his input.

At various stages of writing, I shared copies of my manuscript with the contributors to [Afterthoughts] Part VII of this book. To Andy Macfarlan M.D., Susan Weiss, Tommy Hexter, Al Mermelstein, and Greg Pudhorodsky M.D., I owe a deep measure of gratitude. Not only did they share their time and talent to write Part VII of this book, they provided additional input for clarity and meaning to the reader.

A special thank-you to our daughter, Beth Scanlon for suggesting art for the cover conveying the message of the book. A thank you to Denise Hood of Creative Juices who took Beth's ideas and created the cover.

A blessing for me is God's gift of bringing Monica into my life. For 62 years she has been a steadfast partner and supporter of my endeavors. At times when I became impatient or discouraged, she calms my impatience and dampens my discouragement with support and confidence. Monica is my best friend and we have walked hand in hand over the years. I thank God each day that I wake to see her at my side.

Introduction

A few years ago, I was at a day-long retreat focused on reflection and spiritual growth during the Lenten season. The Beatitudes were the primary topic of discussion. Part of the day was devoted to group discussion, lectures, and time for personal reflection. I was in the library for reflection after participating in a group discussion when I noticed a book title on the shelf that captured my interest. The book was titled *Stages of Faith* by James Fowler. When I opened the book the introduction set the hook; I had to read further. It described a person in the dark of night on his death bed with family surrounding him. In the author's words, *"In that moment of unprecedented aloneness"* in a semi-conscious state of mind, he could sense the people there but *"in this moment like vague memories of people I had once known."* He knew death was near.

At the end of his book, he listed a number of penetrating questions that set the hook deeper into my heart. James Fowler's words reminded me, yes you too are going to be in that bed on some dark night with some of the same thoughts going through your semiconscious mind. James Fowler's book is just one of plenty of reminders of our mortality, *that it will not always be someone else.* This message frequently comes to me through a quote I read or wisdom shared by others. The following are some that may be a message for you.

At a presentation given by Dr. James Avery, he talked about an experience he had at the bedside of a person who was dying. The person told Dr. Avery he was losing his dignity. Dignity is self respect, worthiness, rank or office, title, appreciation of formality, our God given gifts, our job, title, degree, material values. When it is you losing your dignity is when you will realize that the persons around you are slipping away, one by one, like an article of clothing, piece by piece, till you are left naked.

My spiritual director, Msgr. Chester Michael said, "The only things you will take with you when you die are the good deeds you did for others." It's about growing our capacity for love, a recognition of pain and suffering, a positive attitude, acceptance, trust that there is a purpose to life.

In Kathleen Dowling's book *The Grace in Dying*, she talks about our *dual personalities*. She is talking about *moving those values that are in our head, to values that are in our heart.*

What are James Avery, Msgr. Chester Michael, and Kathleen Dowling all saying to me? I hear their messages say to do my best each day, accept the cards dealt to me. *To do the work required getting to know the real me.* It's about a positive recognition of pain and suffering, to pray for strength to endure it, and don't play the waiting game, thinking, it will always be somebody else.

The more messages I read, a similar message resonates. I hope one of these messages speaks to you also. Thomas Merton, and Richard Rohr are a couple of my favorites.

> *"The way to find the real 'world' is not merely to measure and observe what is outside us, but to discover our own inner ground. For that is where the world is, first of all: in my deepest self."*
>
> Thomas Merton

> *"Our life, as individual persons and as members of a perplexed and struggling race, provokes us with the evidence that [life] must have meaning. Part of the meaning still escapes us. Yet our purpose in life is to discover this meaning, and live according to it. We have, therefore, something to live for."*
>
> Thomas Merton

Any way you look at it, the more transparent and vulnerable we become, it will help to break down the pattern of dualistic thinking that is so prevalent in our lives. *Our ego lives in our mind — our true self lives in our heart.*

> *"The mind is given pre-eminence in almost all people. The mind starts steering, judging, analyzing, fixing, controlling, and trying to dominate body and soul. Most people think they are thinking! That's what contemplation can help you resolve. It allows you to find the deeper self—prior to thinking about it, prior to judgments you make and the preferences you have and the endless mental commentary on everything."*
>
> Richard Rohr

> *"It really doesn't matter what you think about things, believe it or not. This is a revolutionary and humiliating breakthrough for most people. What matters is* **What Is.** *"*
>
> Richard Rohr

The message shared in all these comments is to remember that the root of dualistic thinking is **our ego** living in our head, the **true me**, the **"what is"** that lives in our heart. Eventually tomorrow becomes today.

Embrace the task, to become the real me—the true me

Part I:
Finding the Real Me

"Life can only be understood backwards; but it must be lived forwards." ...

Author unknown

On a quest to grow spiritually I developed a template that has led me to discover more about the real me. The four elements to the template are *the MBTI, the Enneagram, and dialogue with penetrating questions about life, and writing about your life shaping experiences (your life story)*.

Working with this template led me to make a commitment to move thoughts in the head to the heart, where our *real me* lives! The template helps me to attain awareness, to engage critical thinking, reminding and edging me to my *true self.* Many of my actions are ego driven by my false self, not the real me. This discovery has changed my worldview and I now realize much of my pain has been caused by not knowing or loving the real me.

> *"Most of us have lived our whole lives with a steady stream of consciousness, with a continual flow of ideas, images, and feelings. And at every moment of our lives we cling to these thoughts and sensations, so much so that I don't have the idea; the idea has me. I don't have the feeling; the feeling has me. We have to discover who this "I" really is, the one who has these always passing feelings and thoughts. Who am I behind my thoughts and feelings? The fixed point that watches things pass through me—is the real ME!"*
>
> Richard Rohr

Turning a blind eye to making a commitment to learning more about the real you is like those of us who say we don't like Brussels sprouts, but have never tried them. Contemplation and study, and finding the real me, is not a high priority on everyone's bucket list. Some people just don't want to go there. Once we buy into the fact that all have dual personalities, we have taken a major step in the right direction. It is then we recognize our ego for what it is. The wearing of many masks for each occasion.

Growing mature spiritually is not easy. The world we live in is constantly evolving and our resistance to change is supported by our ego. The ego living in our head will always resist change and not want to give up control. The ego feeds on stability and superiority, and ignores or misinterprets all that is visible around it.

It doesn't take a rocket scientist to realize we are just a speck of star dust in relationship to the universe. A speck of star dust we may be, it is important to grow our spiritual being, in other words, *"becoming more fully human."*

In their book, *Journey of the Universe*, philosopher Brian Swimme and historian Mary Evelyn Tucker write:

> *"With our empirical observations expanded by modern science, we are now realizing that our universe is a single immense energy event that began as a tiny speck that has unfolded over time to become galaxies and stars, palms and pelicans, the music of Bach, and each of us alive today. The . . . universe is not simply a place but a story—a story in which we are immersed, to which we belong, and out of which we arose.*
>
> *This story has the power to awaken us more deeply to who we are. For just as the Milky Way is the universe in the form of a galaxy, and an orchid is the universe in the form of a flower, we are the universe in the form of a human. And every time we are drawn to look up into the night sky and reflect on the awesome beauty of the universe, we are actually the universe reflecting on itself.*
>
> *With the emergence of humans, we have arrived at an evolutionary breakthrough for being able to develop compassion, not just for our offspring, but for all beings of every order of existence. . . .*
>
> *Our human destiny is to become the heart of the universe that embraces the whole of the Earth community. We are just a speck in the universe, but we are beings with the capacity to feel comprehensive compassion in the midst of an ocean of intimacy. That is the direction of our becoming more fully human."*

"Being a human being is a given; being human is a variable."

Elias Awad

We come from different environments and cultures. We live with the choices we make every day. My commitment is to enhance and modify my values and worldview. Prayerfully I hope to grow my unconditional love for others.

As the lyrics to a hymn by Bob Dufford says, *"Love one another as I have loved you, care for each other, as I have cared for you. Bear each other's burdens, bind each other's wounds, so you will know my return."*

Regardless of our traits, temperaments, culture, religion, or lack of religion, most of us buy into the Golden rule, *"Do unto others as you would have them do unto you."* That is becoming "more fully human." It is to discover the real me behind all those masks. They are ones we put on each day, or maybe we even change the mask several times a day for special situations. The mask maker is living in our head. The mask maker's name is Mr./ Ms. Ego. Mr./Ms. Ego is the person making all the masks. Trying something different can be challenging, but if we don't try something different, we may never know if it could have been rewarding.

The MBTI and the Enneagram have served me as a template or tools, to assist me in my commitment to move those thoughts in my head to my heart. The study and reflection of our traits, temperament, dialoguing with the penetrating questions about life, then writing about your life shaping experiences and relationships [your life story], will help you find your "true self." This is a place some of you may not want to go, but it's very important. It will change your worldview.

To discover and delve into our traits and temperaments, then interact with the penetrating life meaning questions, will shine a light on the Fruit for a transformed worldview.

Temperaments

Where people focus their attention

Some prefer to live in a world focused on people and things around them. Others focus more on the inner world, ideas and impressions.

Ways people look at things

You may be one to view situations based on present experience and trusted info from what you sense or you could be one who tends to base decisions on the future with a view towards patterns and possibilities.

How people decide

Decisions made by some are based on logic and objective analysis. Others tend to make decisions based on values and subjective evaluations.

How we deal with the world we live in

Some prefer a planned, organized approach to life. Others are flexible and spontaneous in their approach to life.

The more we know and grow we not only get insight to who we are but understand the actions and decisions of others.

"Why Not Go Out on a Limb? That's Where All the Fruit Is"
Will Rogers

MBTI —Temperament

"Whatever the circumstances of your life, the understanding of type can make your perceptions clearer, your judgements sounder, and your life closer to your heart's desire."
Isabel Briggs Myers

I have found value in the MBTI, seeing it as a companion to the Enneagram. The MBTI has four basic temperaments. I have read that some who have studied both the Enneagram and the MBTI feel the four temperaments align or complement the nine traits in the Enneagram. The following is their suggested alignment. I am not suggesting all would agree with this assumption; however, I see value in both for growth in my journey searching for the *true self*. I encourage you to discover for yourself.

SJ: 1-2-3-5-6-8-9   NF: 1-2-3-4-5-6-7-8-9

SP: 1-2-3-4-7-8-9   NT: 1-3-4-5-7-8-9

I am sure many have had some experience with the MBTI. It has been used widely in many organizations. Looking at the components of the MBTI I can see a common thread with the Enneagram.

The four dichotomies of the MBTI structure reveal your preferences chosen when taking the discovery test. Each dichotomy has an opposite preference as listed.

E-extraversion-*focus outer world, people and things.*
I-introversion-*focus inner world ideas/impressions.*

S-sensing-*focus present, concrete info from senses.*
N-intuition-*focus future, view patterns & possibilities.*

T-thinking-*decision based on logic, cause and effect.*
F-feeling-*decision based on values subjective personal concerns.*

J-judging-*like planned organized approach.*
P-perceiving-*flexible spontaneous options open.*

The analysis clarifies your preferences or temperament as being slight, moderate, clear or very clear.

My temperament is ESFJ and I scored the following:

Extraversion— Clear

Sensing—Moderate

Feeling/Thinking—Slight (tie score on both)

Judging—Very clear

As an eight on the Enneagram you can see my SJ temperament does seem to support each other as some suggest.

A factor to remember is, the deeper you go, the more you will know.

The MBTI (Meyers-Briggs type Indicator) has been used by many organizations to identify and help people recognize that people differ in temperament and behavior. If you have taken the MBTI you may remember your type, defining how you deal with the outer world.

In David Keirsey's & Marilyn Bates' book, *Please Understand Me* they emphasize the point that we all are different. No matter how hard we try or think we can change others, they are not going to change. The book points out we are different in fundamental ways. We want different things.

We *"believe differently: think, cognize, conceptualize, perceive, understand, comprehend and cogitate differently"*. The book goes on to say, *"For it is the thinking and wanting that is required to change the thinking and wanting. Form cannot be changed."*

I would suggest reading the book *Please Understand Me* by David Keirsey & Marilyn Bates.

Go to meyersbriggs.org to learn more about the MBTI. There are a number of sites online where you can gain additional information about temperament online free. If you want to discover more about your temperament, I would suggest you explore ordering the detailed offering on the next page.

DISCOVER YOUR MBTI (mbtionline.com)

- MBTI® ASSESSMENT
  Take the official Myers-Briggs Type Indicator® assessment. 93 questions, 15 minutes.
- PERSONALITY TYPE REPORT
  Receive your results and a downloadable report providing an overview of your four-letter type.
- LEARNING + PERSONALITY TYPE VERIFICATION
  Walk through an interactive learning session and verify your best-fit
- MBTI® TYPE EXPLORER

The Enneagram — Traits

The Enneagram is showing us that the ego is trying to love itself, but in many ways it has to fail because the ego isn't made of love.
Robert Holden

The Enneagram may not be known as well to as many people as the MBTI. The MBTI relates to our temperament but the Enneagram relates to our traits.

People are different from one another and no amount of trying to change them is going to change anyone. Nor is there any reason to change them, because the differences are probably good, not bad. I am confident there is a relationship between our traits and temperament. Together they paint an expansive blueprint of the real me.

The Enneagram defines nine different traits. Those that are God given traits and those that provide growth opportunities for us. The Enneagram does not label behavior as sin, good or bad, but it provides insights. I would say the Enneagram exposes what is real and what is not. These insights give us new eyes to see through a window [our ego] that may now be fogged.

We all have a core or dominant trait. Mine is an eight. At my worst I can be blunt and domineering, I would say a *"my way or the highway guy, gut decision guy"* and more. One who exemplifies the desire to be independent to pursue their own destiny. A more detailed description would be:

Generally - *strong, assertive, resourceful, independent, determined, action-oriented, pragmatic, competitive, straight-talking, shrewd, and insistent.*

Get into conflicts by being - *blunt, willful, domineering, forceful, defiant, confrontational, bad tempered, rageful, cynical, and vengeful.*

At best Eights are - *honorable, heroic, empowering, generous, gentle, constructive, initiating, decisive, and inspiring.*

This behavior produces a wealth of insights. My need is to recognize that the world is not a battleground, a test of wills, and to recognize my real strength is in vulnerability and openness. An eight at their best can be empowering, gentle and constructive. They can be caring, warm and thoughtful. Balancing of my traits is a growth experience.

However, we all are more than our core or dominant trait. I am not just an eight. I am part of all the other traits. Some may analyze my test scores as something other than an eight. My response is, I see enough insight to myself in an eight to work on.

My Enneagram Test scored me as:

(8) The Challenger 22

(2) Helper & (1) Reformer 19

(3) Achiever 18

(6) Loyalist & (9) Peacemaker 16

(4) Individualist 14

(5) Investigator & (7) Enthusiast 10

A couple stories I can share that authenticate the value of the template are about my relationships with others. I am a Roman Catholic, maybe a level 3 or 4 faith level. Someone very close to me approached me to share that they were agnostic. At the time I was at a level 2-3 faith level, 45 years old, always a hard worker, achieved professional goals, life was good. I am part of a generation born to those who lived through the Depression of the 1930's [born in 1937]. A generation that had values of Family, God, and Country. At the age of 45 I was not thinking about knowing *"the real me"*.

I was thinking about success and survival as defined by American culture. My response to this news was blunt and domineering, an eight on the Enneagram at their worst. Mistakes can be forgiven, but not easily forgot. My response caused pain and our relationship suffered by my behavior. If I would have showed up that day, being gentle, constructive and empowering [my best eight] how different the outcome would have been.

The second example is about a performance evaluation where the person I reported to made a comment that I was insecure. I returned to my office and remarked to my colleague, "Can you believe what Dick said? He said I am insecure." We both laughed, the comment didn't sound like me to either of us. My professional work mask hid the insecurity well to most. The comment stayed fresh in my mind, and in time I realized Dick was right, I was insecure. My formal education ended with high school and 90 percent of the persons reporting to me were college graduates, one a PhD. The first step in growth is to recognize and accept the truth.

I share these stories because they were positive lessons and a growth experience. Knowing more about who we are is a growing experience.

Working with this template has helped me understand my traits and temperament and those of others. Being our best is the high road.

"Most of us have lived our whole lives with a steady stream of consciousness, with a continual flow of ideas, images, and feelings. And at every moment of our lives we cling to these thoughts and sensations, so much so that I don't have the idea; the idea has me. I don't have the feeling; the feeling has me. We have to discover who this "I" really is, the one who has these always passing feelings and thoughts. Who am I behind my thoughts and feelings? The fixed point that watches things pass through me—is the real ME!"

Richard Rohr

As a starter I recommend you go online to the Ennegram Institute (www.enneagraminstitute.com) for a wealth of information. I would suggest you take their test to find out more about yourself. They have a free test and a test for $12.00, the one I would recommend.

* INTRODUCTION TO THE ENNEGRAM
introduction information from their website: *(www.enneagraminstitute.com)*

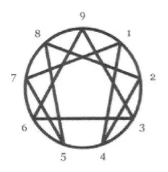

Type One: The Perfectionist
Type Two: The Giver
Type Three: The Performer
Type Four: The Tragic Romantic
Type Five: The Observer
Type Six: The Devil's Advocate
Type Seven: The Epicure
Type Eight: The Boss
Type Nine: The Mediator

Penetrating Questions

How much do you want to share with the ones who care?

"There is no way to penetrate the surface of life but by attacking it earnestly at a particular point."

Charles Horton Cooley

Dialoguing with the penetrating questions establishes the foundation for reflection on our life story, our experiences and relationships. Knowledge and an understanding of our temperament and traits add a new dimension to contemplation.

Some say it is taboo to talk about religion. I know my parents were religious, but I can only guess how their religion related to faith. For me faith and religion are not the same. Some will say there are no answers to these penetrating questions. Some people accept only answers coming from their intellect, not from their heart.

The dialogue to questions in this section are my responses from James Fowler's book *Stages of Faith*. What I write in this book is dynamic. When I revisit the questions as I grow, so the dialogue changes. It is like using your iPhone or computer. If you don't upgrade the app or software you stop learning and stay in the same old mode or rut. You stop learning and growing. Dialoguing with the questions can strengthen our faith and transform our worldview. It has transformed mine to a worldview I can live and die with.

"As a child, I often wondered, 'Who are we? What is the meaning of life?' These questions made me realize that life is what has meaning - not just individual lives, but all of our lives"

Reid Hoffman

Questions from James Fowler's Book, *Stages of Faith*
Life-Shaping Experiences and Relationships

- At present, what relationships seem most important for your life?

- You did/did not mention your father in your mentioning of significant relationships.

- When you think of your father as he was during the time you were a child, what stands out? What was his work? What were his special interests? Was he a religious person?

- When you think of your mother...[same questions]?

- Have your perceptions of your parents changed since you were a child? How?

- Are there other persons who at earlier times or in the present have been significant in the shaping of your outlook on life?

- Have you experienced losses, crises of suffering that have changed or "colored" your life in special ways?

- Have you had moments of joy, ecstasy, peak experiences of break throughs that have shaped your outlook on life in special ways?

- What were the taboos in your early life? How have you lived with or out of those taboos? Can you indicate how the taboos in life have changed? What are the taboos now? What experiences have affirmed your sense of meaning of life? What experiences have shaken or disturbed your sense of meaning of life?

Present Values and Commitments

- Can you describe the beliefs and values or attitudes that are most important in guiding your life?

- What is the purpose of human life?

- Do you feel that some approaches to life are more "true" or right than others? Are there some beliefs or values that all or most people ought to hold and act on?

- Are there symbols or images or rituals that are an important support for your values and beliefs?

- You have described some beliefs and values that have become important to you. How important are they? In what ways do these beliefs and values find expression in your life? Can you give some specific examples of how they have had an effect?

- When you have an important decision or choice to make regarding your life, how do you go about deciding?

- Is there a "plan" for human lives? Are we —individually or as a species—determined or affected in our lives by a power beyond human control?

- When life seems most discouraging and hopeless, what holds you up or renews your hope?

- When you think of the future, what makes you feel most anxious or uneasy (for yourself and those you love, for society or institutions, for the world)?

- What does death mean to you? What becomes of us when we die?

- Why do some persons and groups suffer more than others?

- Some people believe that we will always have poor people among us, and that in general life rewards people according to their efforts. What are your feelings about this?

- Do you feel that human life on this planet will go on indefinitely, or do you think it is about to end?

Religion and Faith

- Do you have or have you had important religious experiences?

- What feeling do you have when you think about God?

- Do you consider yourself a religious person?

- If you pray, what do you feel is going on when you pray?

- Do you feel that your religious outlook is "true?" In what sense?

Are other religious traditions other than yours "true?"

- What is sin (or sins)? How have your feelings about this changed? How did you feel or think about sin as a child, an adolescent, and so on?

- Some people believe that without religion, mortality breaks down. What do you feel about this?

- Where do you feel that you are changing, growing, struggling or wrestling with doubt in your life at the present time? Where is your growing edge?

- What is your mature image (or idea) of mature faith?

"You're a puzzle not only to yourself but also to everyone else, and the great mystery of our time is how we penetrate this puzzle."
Theodore Zeldin

Part II:
Life-Shaping Experiences & Relationships

Do the following questions
inspire you to dialogue with your heart?

I am sharing my thoughts and dialogue with questions from James Fowler's book *Stages of Faith*. I have answered them with a sense that there is no right or wrong answer, they are my answers. Some may say, "There is no answer for some of the questions." My dialogue is here for all to see and makes me vulnerable. Reflection on my dialogue augments my search for the true me. My reflections will change as I grow closer to God. It is not a static dialogue. It is ongoing till my death.

> *"We learn more by looking for the answers to a question and not finding it, than we do from learning the answer itself."*
> Lloyd Alexander
> *[Maybe this is true.]*

Journaling and reflecting on how I answered the questions I asked myself, I consider which of my answers come from my head and which come from my heart. My hope is that my key strokes composing my answers were guided by God, the spirit within me, and prayerfully promotes clarity and growth to the true self.

It is easy to talk about nothing, but hard to talk about the big questions that are important. Why are we here? What is the universe all about? What or who is behind it all? People find it hard to share thoughts on faith, religion, relationships and more. We seem to avoid the big questions. We are so busy about so many things that it is easy to escape from what truly matters.

Does answering these questions and sharing my thoughts with any eyes that want to read them make me feel defenseless? Yes, it makes me very vulnerable; however, the exercise of writing and reflecting on my answers many times over can give me peace, support and growth. It does take commitment and courage and you may want to do the same for yourself and the ones you love.

"The truth is, our own ego-based sense of ourselves is afraid to open to unknown depths, transcending its circle of influence and control."

Richard Rohr

When journaling and meditating, opening our hearts and minds to the questions, our written dialogue can be fruitful. It is interesting how our dialogue reflects our temperament, traits and personality. This reflection, with contemplation, will be helpful to move yourself to a better place. Not to the head, but to the heart. Personally it's a gift and guide for the remaining days of my life.

"People may spend their whole lives climbing the ladder of success only to find, once they reach the top, that the ladder is leaning against the wrong wall."

Thomas Merton

This search for your inner-self will help you find the real fruit on the limb, the real you, that will transform your worldview. A worldview you can live and die with. Change is not what happens outside us; rather, change must first take root within us. We should welcome change as the very sign of life.—This is my dialogue.

◆ *At present, what relationships seem most important for your life?*

At the age of 81 I have been blessed with years of life, experience and wisdom that influence my many choices. Relationships with family and God are on the top of my list now. My wife Monica and I have been married 61 years. She is the mother of our children and our daughter is the mother of our grandchildren. Living in environments and friendships with similar values has been important in my life. In my youth relationships were more activity-based than career-based. From youth to the present day, each relationship along the way has been important.

My relationship with God has grown over the years and I am blessed to come to an understanding that it is all about others, not about me. Father Chet Michael and Father Richard Rohr are the persons who put me on a path of understanding that it's about love.

> *"We are all born to love. It is the principle existence, and its only end."*
>
> Benjamin Disraeli

◆ *You did (did not) mention your father in your mentioning of significant relationships?*

An interesting question, no, I didn't mention my father. Reflection on my choice of persons mentioned all seem to have something in common.

I don't know why I didn't mention Dad. This will require more meditation. My current focus is family, growth and change in my adult life, but not on my youth. My Granddaughter recently asked me *"Papa, what is your first memory as a child?"* Nothing flashed into  my mind at the time when she asked me, and I didn't have a specific answer then or now. Her question did stick in my mind and I have often thought of it. My parents, my sister and brother are all gone and I am the last living member of our family. I can say that when they were living we stayed in touch and I have many happy memories of those times and am glad we did make time for each other.

◆ *When you think of your father as he was during the time you were a child, what stands out? What was his work? What were his special interests?*

One of the foremost thoughts then, and I still reflect on today, are the positive lessons and examples of my parents that are a part of me and my life today.

Dad was one of 17 children, 14 who grew to be adults. Being a part of a large family had to have its own special dynamics. Living in the early 1900's on a farm in Nebraska adds to the uniqueness of his environment. Now add the German immigrant culture and values of the community he lived in and you are not talking about a life in New York City! Can you imagine the difference of a life in New York City to the plains of Nebraska in the early 1900's?

Exposure to current news of the happenings in the world would be delayed by weeks or not reported at all. Your social circle was a few farmers with a similar ethnic background. There were no Broadway productions to see or choices of restaurants to eat at. Roads were not paved. They were dirt changing to mud when it rained. There was no electricity or indoor plumbing. So you can tell, living on the plains of Nebraska was not New York City!

Dad was the youngest of six boys. The oldest boy in the family was to be looked up to by the younger boys and follow his instructions or wishes. It is not uncommon to desire to change the perceived negative experiences we have as a child in the formation of our own family. I gathered from comments Dad made that he longed for more of a relationship of friendship with his brothers, and he tried to create that experience with my brother and me.

Dad's family and the farm community around him were all German Lutherans. They all went to the parochial school next to the church. It was not uncommon for formal education to end with the 8th grade. Dad did not complete his 8th grade. He said he did not go beyond the 4th grade, but I find that hard to believe. He loved to read, and had a great memory. In many ways he was a self-taught person.

Formal education came second to work in the fields. Dad never traveled far from the community where he lived until he was in his 20's; then maybe only as far as Omaha about 100 miles from the farm where he was born. His family did not have an automobile until he was in his late teens. They had four ponies to ride as well as a number of work horses for field work. I recall him saying he and his sister Dora went by horseback to a town 12 miles from home for entertainment. They went to silent movies.

A special treat for him was when traveling vaudeville shows would come to town for a performance. He memorized the jokes and poems that he would hear at these shows. The following is one I heard him recite many times: *A Persian cat perfumed and fair, strayed out through the kitchen door for air, when a tom cat lean and strong, dirty and yellow, came along. He sniffed at the perfumed Persian cat, as he strutted about, and thinking a bit of time to pass, he whispered "kiddo, you have class."*

"That is fitting and proper" was her reply, as she arched the whiskers over her eye. "I'm ribboned, and I sleep on a pillow of silk, and they bathe me daily in certified milk. I'm eating the best food that can be bought, I ought to be happy, but happy I'm not. I ought to be joyful, yes joyful indeed, for really I am highly pedigreed."

The tom cat said to her with a smile, "Come and trust your new found friend for a while. You need to escape from your backyard fence, what you need my dear is experience."

The morning after the night before, the cat came home at the hour of four. The look in her innocent eyes was gone, but the smile on her face was a smile of content. In the after days when the children came, to the Persian cat of pedigreed fame, they were not Persian, they were black and tan, and she told them their dad was a traveling man.

Dad had a quick wit and was seldom found without a fast remark; many times just funny. His comments could be hurtful like, *"Your hat is too small for your head"* to one whose ego was super-sized.

His comments could also be humorous. One time when he was visiting me in Virginia where the roads wind through wooded areas and over rolling hills, he commented, *"I think they just dropped the asphalt behind the cows on their way to the barn when it was time to pave these roads."*

In the fall of 1985 I purchased a new Alfa convertible that I was so proud of, as I had dreamt of having a convertible for a long time. A short time after I had it my parents came to visit. I was eager to take my Dad for a ride in the new convertible.

After a ride through the countryside with the top down, we arrived home and I asked Dad, *"What do you think of my new car?"* His response: *"I wouldn't have the damn thing if you gave it to me."* I said *"Why do you say that, Dad?"* His response: *"Because you can't get in it—and you can't get out of it!"*

The comment, while a bit hurtful at the time and yet humorous and, was certainly true for him at the age of 85. I must admit that once I reached the age of 65, I thought of my Dad every time I got in the car and out of the car. With a smile I would think to myself, Dad was right, this car is hard to get into—and each time I drove the car, it was getting harder to get out of it! Dad was not a materialistic person. He was happy with what God gave him and loved his family and others.

◆ *When you think of your mother, same questions?*

Mom was born June 3, 1909. She was nine years younger than dad. Growing up in a small town in Nebraska her life was different than Dad's. Being one of six children, and not one of 14 like Dad, was different for starters. While there were responsibilities and plenty of work to do in the garden, it was not the same as growing up on

a large farm. Her parents' acreage was located on the edge of town with acres of strawberries to pick, sweet corn and vegetables to weed and care for. Mom went to the public school and it was more common to finish high school than living on the farm.

Mom was a good student as I recall listening to her stories about school. They left me with the impression that Mom liked school. She talked about being a finalist in spelling bees and liking algebra. A formal education for a female was not one that was encouraged in all families in the early 1900's.

She talked about playing baseball with her four brothers—three older—and her family life was simple; it centered both around the German Lutheran church in town and work to be done at home. When she was a young girl she went to the Dempster Mill Manufacturing Company by horse and buggy to pick her dad up after work. I am not sure if she drove the buggy or it was one of her brothers. A real treat was getting a sack of hard candy from her dad's check on payday.

Mom's parents never owned a car. They walked or took a horse and buggy. Later, as the garden grew, the same horse and buggy was used to sell produce door-to-door and to make deliveries to the local grocery stores. Her mother let her keep the pennies paid by customers for produce orders. Those pennies saved helped her purchase a new bicycle for $15.

Mom was close to her brother John. Because he was five years older than Mom, her parents considered it acceptable for her to go to events with him. He took her to dances and social events; many of the social activities were at church. My parents' first date was at church. Mom introduced her brother John to dad's sister Ida. John and Ida married a month after my parents were married.

Mom had a very strong work ethic and an unshakable faith in God. She had a passion regarding her faith. She was a religious person and dedicated to her church. She had a perfect attendance record for Sunday School for seven years. Never idle, Mom was very productive and also never complained. She had a very strong will, but was definitely a giver, not a taker.

One of my most cherished memories of Mom is her frequent

expression of prayer while working—singing hymns as she was baking bread, crocheting an afghan, or cleaning the house. Listening to her sing her favorite hymns while doing her work was a sincere expression of her faith and love of God.

No one was with Mom when she died and I have always felt sad about that. I still feel guilty that I did not get back to Nebraska before she died. Dad, brother, and sister all went home that evening from the hospital not knowing how serious her condition was. She died without any member of her family present—November 3, 1990— the date of her grandson Tom's birthday.

I always thought my makeup was more like my mother's than like Dad's. Looking back I realize that I'm a blend of both. I have my mother's strong will, but I have many of Dad's traits too.

For me, it was helpful to use journaling techniques as I was seeking a deeper understanding of my relationship with my parents. A good tool for me was using a written dialogue with a person significant to me, in this case my parents. It is interesting to compare the two dialogues that show how our relationships differed. They both touched me deeply and still bring me comfort and peace.

This is the written dialogue I journaled with my mother.

May 8, 1998

I miss you Mom, and I am sorry I could not be with you, when you passed from this life to the next. *"That's okay sonny boy, it is not all that much anyway. You nor I knew it was time for me to go."* I would like to know what it is like where you are. I feel your presence in and around me many times. *"I am what I was and will be forever more. I will live in you, your children, grandchildren and those after to come.*

Try hard to grow in knowledge and love. Then we, too, can become one. It is not what is there or here to worry about, you put your trust in God and put away all your doubts." Thank you, Mom, for all your love and sticking with me. Your tender care, your example of strength and unconditional love will always be my cornerstone.

"Who looks outside, dreams, who looks inside, awakes."

Carl G. Jung

Journaling with my dad:

May 9, 1998

"Time has passed and events are gone, but our memories stay, as our lives travel on. You did what you thought was right but it was not always right for the time. It was not always right for me, then or any time. I adopted some of your traits, hopefully good as well as some of the bad. Your put down humor is one I wish you or I never had. You didn't have the slightest idea of what you did. You thought you were funny, but you hurt so many. You made them sad. Your mind is scattered now, your body is weak. It is too late to talk about it now, so we will let it all sleep. I will honor you now and evermore, by not putting others down, to be the town clown."

I never compared the journaling entries next to each other with Mom and Dad before. The difference is quite interesting. There is a dialogue taking place with my mother, one that brings tears to my eyes each time I read it. It seems so real, that she is with me at that moment. With Dad there is criticism in my words, no dialogue, it is written in a rhyming fashion [like Dad would do]. I see so much of me in him with my journaling.

I have always loved this photo of my parents. The lyrics of their song says so much about them. It was never about stuff, it was about love.

"We ain't got a barrel of money, maybe we're ragged and funny, but we're traveling along, singing a song, side by side."

♦ *Have your perceptions of your parents changed since you were a child? How?*

Not really, I had a happy childhood. When joining the Navy at 17, I was introduced to the world, a world so much larger than the southeast corner of Nebraska. Joining the Navy I was on my own. Many times I felt like I was government property, but kind of independent. [I did have to call everyone Sir.] I had thoughts about how my future life might change after I got out of the Navy. I always wanted to be a farmer and thought when I was discharged farming would be my vocation. As it turned out, as with many plans, plans change.

Even though my independent personality sparked disagreements with my parents, when my hurtful actions from time to time caused pain, forgiveness and love were the winners. We have always been family and I am grateful for that. As my career took me from Nebraska to Missouri, New York, Virginia, Pennsylvania and back to Virginia we stayed in touch. We would visit my parents at least once a year if not more and they would visit us at least once a year if not more. Today, I cherish those memories. I love my parents and know they both always loved me, as a youth and as an adult. I guess I may have made it difficult at times.

♦ *Are there other persons who at earlier times or in the present have been significant in the shaping of your outlook on life?*

Monsignor Chester P. Michael was a person who had a major influence on my life. The first sentence of the introduction to the book he wrote with Marie Norrisey, Arise, speaks loud to the influence he had on my life-shaping experiences. The central idea of their book is that, *"The key to a successful,*

happy life is the fullest possible development of our unlimited potential of love." This has become the guiding principle for my life.

Monsignor was my spiritual director for many years and I attended a two year program, [SDI] Spiritual Direction Institute. He conducted the course along with Marie Norrisey. During the two years they shared some 50 tools for spiritual growth. The two tools, the (MBTI) Myers-Briggs Type Indicator, and the Enneagram, especially the Enneagram, have provided me such depth to the real person I am.

Books written by authors Richard Rohr and Thomas Merton are favorites. Others such as Kathleen Dowling, Henri Nouwen, Thomas Keating, Walter Wink, M. Scott Peck have influenced my thoughts. The book, *Seeds of Contemplation,* was one of the first Merton books I read. Many of the thoughts shared by Merton are serious and penetrating, but are expressed in a way that resonates with my soul. I can continue to rely on this book each time I read it to find additional growth. I can meditate on just one sentence for a long while. A thought Merton shared in this book is, *"Our idea of God tells us more about ourselves than about Him."* I find a lot to think about in that sentence.

◆ *Have you experienced losses, crises or suffering that have changed or "colored" your life in special ways?*

Several thoughts come to mind. One thought is at age 55 being told I had cancer. The other was when my sister died on my birthday, December 24, 2013. When she died I realized I was the last person left in our family.

When I learned I had cancer, I remember the day well when things were not going to stay the way they were. Monica and I were returning to our home from our tax appointment with our CPA in Fairfax, Virginia. My urologist called to inform me that he had the results of my biopsy and requested I come to his office with my wife to discuss the results. That was the one phone call that no one wants to receive, because you know that the news is not going to be good. The doctor told us that I had prostate cancer and the cancer had advanced outside the prostate. In the end, it is what it is, and it will be what we make it.

As I digested the news I cycled through all three of the emotions we hear others do when they get bad news. This time it was not someone else, it was me. The emotions of anger, denial, and fear were all present. I was 55, life was good, and cancer always happened to someone else. I was aware that each year there are thousands of people who got cancer, but why did I turn out to be one of them?

It was when I started living my life with cancer that started my conversion from a materialistic state of mind to seeking more balance in my life, and to enriching my spiritual values. I searched for guidance, a spiritual director, and those actions led me to journaling. Journaling helped me realize the importance of taking some time each day to reach my deeper self.

Whether one is being faced with a serious health issue or any crisis in life, it becomes a time of contemplation. The issue may be divorce, death in the family; for me this time it was prostate cancer. Of course, there is cancer of various degrees of seriousness, and prostate cancer is no exception. For my situation the prostate cancer was serious, as it was discovered after it metastasized outside the prostate. This stage of prostate cancer changes options to consider for treatment.

I try to be positive about any crisis I face in life and feel my attitude towards the crisis is an important element for living with the crisis. I think for me one word to capture or describe an event or crises like this would be *Transforming.*

As a Christian, my faith and religion are guiding principles that keeps me on track with the correct attitude. Realizing that I was not in control of this event was a start to my transformation.

"I wonder if the only way that conversion, enlightenment, and transformation ever happen is by a kind of divine ambush. We have to be caught off guard. As long as you are in control, you are going to keep trying to steer the ship by your previous experience of being in charge."

Richard Rohr

My cancer was an ambush. It was then when I started living my life with cancer and I started seeking more balance in my life and to enrich my spiritual values.

The other suffering and loss that touched me spiritually was when my sister died on my birthday, December 24, 2013. It shouldn't be a shock to me after experiencing my mother's death November 3,1990, my father's August 29, 2000, and my brother's April 1, 2006. Each of these losses were events of sadness. Now I was the last member of our family alive. Betty was the one who encouraged me to pursue more formal education. Her example was one I always looked up to. When you lose those you love, you are reminded of how fast time passes and it strengthened my resolve to grow closer to God.

◆ ***Have you had moments of joy, ecstasy, peak experience or break-throughs that shaped or changed your life?***

Joy comes from events and places when I least expect it. Walking a daughter or son down the aisle on their wedding day, graduation day from college, and having the family home for holidays or celebrations. The older you get the more you realize the value of time and the gift of healthy relationships with family, friends, all you love.

"Every challenge you encounter in life is a fork in the road. You have the choice to choose which way to go - backward, forward, breakdown or breakthrough."

Ifeanyl Enoch Onuoha

Living with cancer over the years has the potential of a breakdown or a break-through. For me it was an opportunity, a second chance to get it right. Not the me that lives in my head, the me that lives in my heart. This event started my journey to the inside, not to hover on the surface of things but to penetrate into the depth of matters. Getting to know the real me.

◆ ***What were taboos in your early life? How have you lived with or out of these taboos? Can you indicate how the taboos in your life have changed? What are the taboos now?***

I think that something taboo is about our attitude toward free thought and expression. Having an open mind to the expression of others does not persuade my choices. Beliefs and values are my guide post.

"The most strongly enforced of all known taboos is the taboo against knowing who or what you really are behind the mask of your apparently separate, independent, and isolated ego."

Alan Watts

In my youth during the '40's, the root of taboos was driven by the same stimulus as they are today. It is what our current society imposes on us. What is acceptable? The labels of taboos have changed since the '40's, but society is still in the driver's seat. The world continues to evolve into a place where the things that we see as being taboo change with society's attitudes. In the 40's Divorce, a Lutheran going to a Catholic church. No one heard of LGBTQ. Our attitudes of taboos can change when we realize we are not the main event in the circus tent.

How I have lived with or without taboos over the years is with respect for others' choices, a strong consideration for balance in life, and respect for the choices made by others. To have commitment to uphold the values and beliefs of my life.

"Live in such a way that you wouldn't be ashamed to sell your parrot to the town gossip."

Will Rogers

◆ **What experiences have affirmed your sense of the meaning of life? What experiences have shaken or disturbed your sense of meaning?**

The more sand that escapes through my hourglass of life, the clearer I see through it. Eighty plus years of life has been bestowed upon me, a lot to see. My life has been blessed with good luck, support and advice from friends and mentors, and an appetite for hard work. This, with the disappointments and failures I have experienced, I am discovering the meaning of life.

What you do for others is what counts. As Father Chet told me, "The only things you will take with you when you die Roger, are the good deeds you did for others."

Disappointments and failures are challenging when they happen. However, they are the greatest lessons for growth. Your attitude, persistence and determination to keep trying is where the best lesson is learned.

Part III:
Present Values & Commitments

*The ultimate value of life depends upon awareness
and the power of contemplation rather than upon
mere survival.*

Aristotle

◆ *Can you describe the beliefs and values or attitudes that are most important in guiding your own life?*

Relationships and spiritual growth in the broader sense are important at this stage of my life. Attaining a deeper level of faith appears to be one of the parts of the puzzle. It is to find the strength to face the challenges of life in a positive way. Finding ways to improve my prayer life, how to practice the presence of God through contemplation. With the help of a spiritual guide in this time of questioning and study of my personal traits and temperament are useful tools for me. Dialoguing with these penetrating questions. It means looking back and knowing where and how I want to go. I feel a need to develop a global consciousness and to bring more balance in my life.

The improvement of my relationships with others will be a goal to my dying day. As an eight on the Enneagram, I need to work on the negative ones that would improve my relationship with others. Let me say the same in another way. Too many of the capital sins—envy, gluttony, anger, pride, greed—can be found listed as negative for an eight on the Enneagram. My growth is dependent on my ability not to be changed, but to be transformed. In change we think of something new or different. In transformation it's about when something old falls apart or lost. I have to work on subtraction of my bad traits and not think of growth as change.

◆ *What is the purpose of human life?*

The words of Msgr. Chester Michael come to mind. *Authenticity—develop a good relationship with yourself, Significance—develop a good relationship with God, Transparency—be open to others, and Solidarity— responsibility to others.* [social justice]

All four attributes are a life-long process of learning. To me, authentic is not to live in my head. Learning not to judge, control, and compare. In times of trouble I am most aware of my need to seek help of those informed, experienced and mature for counsel. I have been fortunate to be guided by the Holy Spirit to those resources. I remain open to the thoughts of not one organization or religion. I don't think that God intended salvation for a small group of insiders. God's love is universal. I feel led by God throughout my life, yet given the free will of choices. The purpose of life is to be transformed through the experiences of my life, and with wisdom as I age. To learn on my journey that it is about spiritual transformation and this must become an actual process of letting go. And along the way, it is prudent to live by the Golden Rule.

> *"I don't believe that God expects all human beings to start from zero and to reinvent the wheel of life in their own small lifetimes. We must build on the common "communion of saints" throughout the ages. This is the inherited fruit and gift, which is sometimes called the wisdom tradition. It is not always inherited simply by belonging to one group or religion. It largely depends on how informed, mature, and experienced your particular teachers are."*
>
> Richard Rohr

◆ *Do you feel that some approaches to life are more "true" or right than others?*

Not really, I think each person is given different gifts and in the lottery of life, those gifts are influenced by different cultures and environments. Discovering and sharing our special gifts with others should be a common goal. As a child we are innocent, unsuspicious of the complicated world we are born into. When we get older we are exposed to the conduct of others and learn most by observation and comparison. When we compare we judge, which leads to feeling and embracing different approaches believed to be more true or right than others.

◆ *Are there some beliefs or values that all or most people "ought" to hold and act on?*

One of the most important actions we all should take is the responsibility to act. *"to get to know your true self, not the person who wears the masks, the one we all show to others."* Actions based on unconditional love should be the foundation of all beliefs and values, motivated by unconditional love. This everyone should hold true. Everyone should strive to model their motivation to act as described in the Golden Rule, the one rule all of us should be able to agree with. It is not about what you say, but why you say it.

The Golden Rule is not...

• values based on rule-following behavior to get to heaven.
• following rules because you are afraid of punishment.
• values based on recognition from others.

Those who are motivated to do good for others because it is true, coming from the heart are living the Golden Rule. Actions from the ego driven head, looking for a reward or recognition, are not. If you live by the Golden Rule you don't have to worry about the rest! Organized religion stressing following the rules—if you do this you get punishment or reward—has their share of responsibility for atheism and agnosticism.

George Bernard Shaw wrote, *"There is only one religion, though there are a hundred versions of it."*

◆ *Are there symbols or images or rituals that are important to you?*

Yes, they are important to me, but only when they add meaning to my worship and I have a clear understanding of what the symbol or ritual represents. I am a Catholic and my religion is rich with rituals and symbols. The origins of many rituals seem connected to previous cultures or other religions. I find this interesting and I embrace the similitudes we share in rituals. The Jewish Shavuot, also known as Pentecost, marks the time the Jews were given the Torah on Mount Sinai. Pentecost to the Christian marks the disciples receiving the Holy Spirit. Mikvah, the Jewish ritual bath, is a rite of purification. The Christian baptism cleanses the believer from sin and puts them on a path of righteousness.

We bless ourselves with Holy Water as we enter the sanctuary to remind us of our baptism. We stand when the gospel is read out of respect for the word. There are many more examples but if I bless myself or stand not being focused or respecting the true reason for the action, they have no value. As with most things in life, balance is important.

Respect for our nation's flag is important. Many people have given their lives and served in many ways to preserve and protect our country's values. Citizens have the liberty and freedom to disagree with what they feel is unjust or should be changed. I think there are many ways to express your feelings or convictions without disrespect for the flag, the symbol representing the country that allows you to do that.

> *"Some people are overly invested in religious ceremonies, rituals, and rules that are all about who's in and who's out. Jesus did not come to create a spiritual elite or an exclusionary system. He invited people to "follow" him by personally bearing the mystery of human death and resurrection. Of itself, this task does not feel "religious," which is why it demands such faith to trust it."*
>
> Richard Rohr

◆ *What relationships or groups are most important as support of your values and beliefs?*

Family, friends, community and the examples set by others who give so much to making the world a better place for all of us to live. I am so blessed to be given the gift to be part of our family. My wife set a high standard and example of love and caring for others with our children. In addition to being a teacher, our daughter has followed in the same shoes her mother wore with her children. Our son's profession as a doctor is one of giving of his gifts for the good of others. It is the mother in our family that has set the atmosphere that grounded and cultivated our family in giving and sharing with others. With respect to friendship, I saw a quote on Facebook that speaks to friendship. *"Family isn't always blood. It's the people in your life who want you in there. The ones who would do anything to see you smile, and who love you no matter what."*

For me that's a friend, it's not about "call me if you need anything." It's being there to give me a hug when there are no words to express the joy or pain. I have been blessed with friends in my life.

Community for me is found in church but I think community can lose its true meaning sometimes in an institution. It is not about following rules and regulations or going to a service station [church] to get a faith fix once a week or on some special day of observance. It's about giving thanks to God for the gift of life every day. Church is a place to gather with others to share in the joy, pain and suffering of life. I find that community in church.

It is unfortunate that there are an increasing number of "Nones" and "Spiritual-but-not-religious"—those who don't identify with a particular religious tradition at all. Many of those feel it is hopeless to try to work within the church to change and improve. When people feel that myths, performing rituals, mouthing prayers or embracing dogma is what going to church is about—this group [the nones] will continue to grow. True love is not about my-way or the highway.

Thomas Merton embraced dialogue with many faith traditions. Every faith contains some truth. If we approach dialogue with the true spirit of ecumenism, we can grow our wisdom and love, whoever we are. Seeking that truth and wisdom is what our dialogue should be about. Dialogue should make us happy, not defensive or aggressive.

◆ *You have described some beliefs and values that have become important to you. How important are they? In what ways do these beliefs and values find expression in your life?*

First, to trust and hope for a better somewhere after death. To strive to improve my relationship with self and others, understanding others' traits and temperaments. It is important to think critically about ourselves as the first step from dualistic mind toward full consciousness. It teaches us rational honesty and patience with ambiguity and mystery.

It has been a life-long season learning through my mistakes and a blessing seeing the magic work in the lives of those living by the Golden Rule. Father Rohr said, *"Hopefully, a time will come when the life of Christ will be so triumphant in us that we care more about others than our own selves, or, better, when there is no longer such a sharp distinction between my self and other selves."*

At 80 years old I would say I am doing repair work on a life that has failed enough times to keep busy just doing patchwork on all I have broken.

Improving my listening skills is one trait I have found valuable to my growth. I truly try to listen to others with my heart before my ego [head] starts judging, critiquing, and computing how I am going to answer.

Those bedfellows, the gang of six, Mr. decisive, judgmental, willful, confrontational, sarcasm, and critical have found a comfortable place to live in my head for the past 80 years. You could say they have developed a good friendship with each other living in my head. Those characters that live in my heart with the Holy

Spirit—contemplation, humility, love, consideration, forgiveness—are the real me.

I have a job on my hands, to reform the ego living in my head with the gang of six. The ones who get in the way to finding the real me. I am sure you have heard said, "You can't learn anything while you are talking."

> *"Silence is the necessary space around things that allows them to develop and flourish without my pushing."*
>
> Richard Rohr

◆ *When you have an important decision or choice to make regarding your life, how do you go about deciding?*

Change in itself just happens, but how I react to each situation is the key to my growth. If I can stay focused on transformation and not make reactionary choices, I can learn and get new meaning to my goal, to be transformed improving my inner life. If I make decisions being judgmental or self-serving, the result many times can be hurtful or destructive to a relationship or goal.

It is not only what I say, but how I say it. As an eight on the Enneagram I have a trait that challenges me every day. My wrongful behavior is hurtful when I reflect on bad choices. In addition, I also have given someone the opportunity to live rent free in my head. Change is going to happen and life is about making choices.

When reflecting on which decisions are important to my life, I think they all are important. A small crack in the dam may not seem significant and can go unnoticed, but when ignored it can grow and become the source of the dam breaking. You have to tend your garden if you want it to grow.

Father Chet Michael often shared the following advice:. *"It is all about keeping the three P's in balance"* (Power, Pleasure and Possessions). They are all good, but when they get out of balance you can easily forget the reason you are on earth. We are here for the transformation of our God given gifts into love, to do good for the most.

> *"Nothing is guaranteed about the future, but we live in hope of being happy."*
>
> The Dalai Lama

Making good choices, living in the moment, are good guidelines for being happy.

◆ ***Is there a "plan" for human lives? Are we—individually or as a species—determined or affected in our lives by power beyond human control?***

I have read the earth is about 14 billion plus years old. That in itself gives reason to look up to the sky and wonder how does this all work and what is my place in the vast universe. I also read there may be one hundred billion or more galaxies. In his book "Astrophysics for People in a Hurry" Neil DeGrasse Tyson shared, *"People who believe they are ignorant of nothing have neither looked for, nor stumbled upon the boundary between what is known and unknown in the universe."*

In reference to faith, Neil DeGrasse Tyson's quote gives everyone, especially those who have been blessed with an exceptional gift [intellect], something to ponder. As an individual, we have the power to influence the outcome of many events in our life by the choices we make. In the context of the universe, we all can feel quite small and humble.

As an individual, there are events beyond understanding we have and control. Why does a person have to suffer with an illness or a child is taken at a young age? These events are beyond human understanding, but we are still left with the choice of how we react to the events. My answer to this question, while I am here on earth, I have an obligation to do the best I can using the talents and gifts given me to love and do good for others. It gets down to this, LOVE.

> *"Each of us has to come together in a unique manifestation point of energy, as a particular being at a particular moment in chronological time, in the world of emergent form, presumably for the purpose of self aware experience and contribution of our gifts to other sentient beings, culminating in transcendence and perhaps co-creation. After a sojourn in the dimension of the material world of form and impermanence, we return to our eternal, unchanging, and absolute Source in both its manifest and unmanifest aspects."*
>
> Richard Rohr

◆ *When life seems most discouraging and hopeless, what holds you up or renews your hope?*

Persistence, 81 years of experience, faith and knowing there is always light at the end of the tunnel, that cultivates my optimism. I also pray for guidance and strength. Not to take the issue away, but for strength to get through the pain and learn a lesson for growth.

On our journey of life we are all strapped to a water wheel, the wheel of life which continues to turn. When we are on the top we are in the sunshine, but as we progress toward the bottom of the wheel we are in the mud. Here's the secret, put some grease on the hub of the wheel to get through the mud faster.

> *"Wherever my story takes me, however dark and difficult the theme, there is always some hope and redemption, not because readers like happy endings, but because I am an optimist at heart. I know the sun will rise in the morning, that there is a light at the end of every tunnel."*
>
> Michael Morpurgo

◆ *When you think about the future, what makes you feel most anxious or uneasy regarding yourself, those you love, society, institutions, the world?*

If I were asked to answer this question in one word, that word would be "change." Myself, as with each generation before and those generations after me, to some degree resist change. As a child growing up on a farm in Nebraska with no iPhone, no internet, and one channel on our black and white TV qualifies me as a person who has witnessed change. On Saturday night I would go with my parents to a village of 600 persons where mom would shop for groceries. Dad and I would go to the implement dealer while mom shopped. The men would gather at the implement dealer while their wives shopped. At the implement dealer world problems were solved, just as some do today at Starbucks.

My father was born November 20, 1900. He lived to see the airplane fly. To watch astronauts land on the moon. Listening to my dad and his friends as a child, change was what made them anxious about the future.

I could listen, but not comment. This is one change not always practiced by the current generation. I knew I was listening to some old folks who just couldn't see the value of change.

I have always remembered those Saturday evenings at the implement dealer, vowing that I would never become a person who resisted change. I knew that change was positive and good. At 81 I am not sure I have honored that commitment.

A Nebraska farm boy in 1947 would have never dreamt what all socially and technically became reality. One thing that is different now is the speed in which change is taking place. Going from the birth of the airplane to landing on the moon is significant [66 years]. During my life technology has changed at such a rapid pace the impact has also been significant on our social atmosphere. Change is reflected in today's society and institutions in the world.

Change in attitude and values. The family unit, divorce, LGBTQ, marriage, race relations, gender equality, spiritual awakening, materialism, a my way or the highway view, religion, secularism are some of the changes many have witnessed in their life time. Technology has played a major role in the development of those changes. Much of this is good for our world when it is rooted in love and respect. When the attitude to change is rooted in, what's in it for me, that attitude isn't good.

I am anxious for the future of our children and grandchildren, hoping they have an open mind to change, that their decisions are balanced with both the past and current values; there is good in both. I am anxious for the institutions with a *"stuck in the mud"* tradition, religious and governmental, that can't seem to catch the virus of unconditional love, to helping others and looking only to protecting their interests.

I am not an idealist, but a realist. One who lives his life in the center of the road, not too far right or not too far left. Close enough to the center to be able to hear and consider both points of view. Not to be extreme, too far left or right. It's all about balance.

It's paying attention to **The Three P's—Power, Pleasure, Possessions.** All three are good but you have to keep their values in balance.

◆ *What does death mean to you? What becomes of us when we die?*

All of us know the door to death is one we all pass through. It is good to know that after death we won't have to worry about taxes every time congress meets.

In any event we are certain death well occur. No one knows when or how, but it will happen. Fear, anger, denial are all real emotions we experience. The sooner we come to acceptance the more natural death becomes. Certainly the exercise of getting to know the "real me" and dialogue with these penetrating questions is an act of preparation for death.

I believe in life after death. Life is eternal, death is a passageway to a new life. More important, love is immortal, and God is love. God's boundless energy of love is for all the world and all the creatures living in it. I don't think life after death is a "my way or the highway" type of thing. There are many paths to the mountain. Best said by my Father Chet, *"The only things you take with you when you die Roger, are the good deeds you did for others."*

What becomes of us when we die is beyond human comprehension; it is about faith. I have read books, listened to testimony of those who have had visions of the afterlife. Some see a bright light, some see deceased relatives, some see God. I do not deny or denounce these events just because I personally have not experienced one. It is my faith in God's immortal love to be committed to love that will carry me on. *"There are three that remain— faith, hope and love—the greatest of these is love."* 1 Corinthians 13:13

> *"The only difference between death and taxes is that death doesn't get worse every time Congress meets."*
>
> Will Rogers

◆ *Why do some persons and groups suffer more than others?*

I have skipped answering this question a number of times because I don't have an answer. Some say it is because it's the way you respond to tragedy and pain. That if you have a positive attitude you will grow from the experience. This is true, but for me that does not answer why do some suffer more than others in the first place? There is no question that we all have our own journey of life to live and we are all going to have pain and suffering of some type along the way. St. Teresa said, *"I know God won't give me anything that I can't handle. I just wish he didn't trust me so much."*

Maybe that is part of the answer why some have more pain than others. It does certainly get back to how we live with the pain and how we turn negative energy into positive energy. I have witnessed those who have suffered loss turn the tragedy into positive energy, and that becomes their focus and gift for others.

◆ *Some people believe that we will always have poor people among us, and that in general life rewards people according to their efforts. What are your feelings about this?*

The good book says, "Do not judge, and you will not be judged, Do not condemn, and you will not be condemned, Grant pardon, and you will be pardoned, Give, and there will be gifts for you....The amount you measure out is the amount you will be given back." That is where the heart of the answer lies. When the world is transformed to unconditional love, yes, that will be the day we have no more poor. To paraphrase Teilhard de Chardin, *"It will be the second time we discover fire."* That would be called heaven on earth.

Yes, some people are poor because of the choices they make. When I see the person standing on the corner by the traffic light with a sign saying "anything will help," my head tells me this person maybe is making a career of begging and at the end of the day he/ she will get into their BMW feeling good about the day's work. They may go buy drugs or alcohol to support their habit. The judging in my head is not positive. They may be victims of choices made, bad luck or someone's actions put them in an unfortunate position. Things happen.

I consciously want to move on from judging others and having more compassion for others. This will be a life-long task for me. It is these attempts at love that lead me to a higher level of love.

Another question is, What are the real rewards of life? Is the real reward about your status or what you accumulate, or is the reward what you share with others? A person I admired said *"Roger, I have never seen a U-Haul behind a hearse."*

If your wealth is your intellect, your status and what you accumulate, you probably are living in your head. If your focus is to rely on doing what is best for others leading you to be compassionate, you probably are living in your heart.

It is about the choices we make helping others, not helping ourselves. We can be smart, have a lot of money and still be poor. We can have little education and no money and be rich. It's about choices and attitudes.

◆ ***Do you feel that human life on this planet will go on indefinitely, or do you think it is about to end?***

I don't have a clue and never think much about it. I would say this is a question for those who live in their head and not in their heart. I do think it is greed and ignorance that drives excessive consumption and waste of the resources of our earth. The food and water that we waste or poison will shorten the life of the planet. It is like knowing smoking is not good for your body, but you keep smoking. Chances are that the smokers will shorten their life. We have to discover that we don't own any part of the planet but recognize that we are part of it. Being part of it we should be good stewards and love our planet and take care of it.

In the overall scheme of the question about the planet or universe, each individual is quite small, but all part of the same universe. Each of us should do our part to conserve.

> *"In the face of catastrophic climate change and global violence, we can give up, give in, or surrender. Once we start on that downward path, we lose our integrity and become our worse selves. But I'm inviting us instead go rise to the occasion and become our best selves!"*
> John Dear - *They will Inherit the Earth*

Part IV:
Religion & Faith

Dare, dream, dance, smile, and sing loudly! And
have faith that love is an unstoppable force!

Suzanne Brockmann

◆ *What can you tell me about your religion and your faith?*

First, I think that faith is a conviction that God can, and it is a hope I have that God will. I am going to take a chance on grace.

Thomas Keating said, *"The primary purpose of religion is to help us move beyond the separate-self sense to union with God."* As a child growing up in Nebraska on a farm, the thought that religion and faith may be something different never crossed my mind. My parents were religious and they provided for me an environment to know right from wrong. I learned that my behavior would result in support and rewards or my behavior could result in disapproval and sometimes punishment. When I was 6 or 7 years old, I picked up a hammer in the garage and started pounding on the fender of the family car. I was not thinking of the consequences that my choice to pound on that fender may bring.

When caught in the act by my father, his response taught me it is better to think before you act. The punishment could be a result of my actions when I make bad choices. Religion taught me bad choices may send me to hell. Good choices may send me to heaven. As a young person I connected religion and faith that way.

Religion can be a head thing if you go to church on Sunday and don't practice love and your faith seven days a week. Faith is a *contemplative* inner experience. Faith is trust, belief, confidence, and conviction.

In my youth religion was practiced at St. John Lutheran Church in Beatrice, Nebraska. The family was immersed in the activities and worship at the church. I remember going as a family in the car to visit people in the community who were not members of our church or regular members of any church. We waited in the car watching dad as he went up to the house and knocked on their door. I can still clearly see him with one hand in his pocket, maybe saying to himself, what am I going to say, maybe saying a prayer while he waited for them to answer the door to invite him in. His goal was to welcome them to be part of the church family and many people did accept his invitation.

Dad's example of reaching out to others has strengthened my resolve to know, "It's not about me, but others." Our church truly was a supportive community that developed healthy relationships and guidance to make positive life choices.

As I grew older, I developed thoughts about the role religion and faith play in my life. Google says, and we all know [Google is always right?]—faith is *"a strong belief in God or in the doctrines of a religion, based on spiritual apprehension rather than proof."--"trust, belief, confidence, conviction."*

My conviction now is that religion and faith are not the same. My religion is an outer experience that provides me a ritualistic, moralistic, doctrinaire pathway. It provides a community with an opportunity to grow in fellowship and love with others and to love *all life* that resides in this world. Religion is only one pathway with others that supports my inner growth.

> *"We all live in the same cycle of unrequested birth and unrequested death. Someone else is clearly in control, yet most of our lives are spent accepting and surrendering to this truth, trusting that this "Someone" is good and trustworthy besides. It is the very shape and journey of faith."*
>
> Richard Rohr

The trajectory of my life is no exception. Someone else is clearly in control. That is at the core of my faith. I regret that I never had conversations with my parents about their faith and how faith related to their religion.

Faith is about our transformation. My life on earth should be more about transformation than conversion. It is not about some transactions made while I am on earth [if you do this you get that]. My transformation is to see a loving God in everyone and everything that exist on earth. *Love is not what you do; it's about your motivation to do it.*

It's been said that our experiences of ordinary life will transform us if we are willing to experience them fully. My prayer is that in my ordinary life I will be transformed to always see God in all.

I love this quote. *"Most people do not see things as they are because they see things as they are!"* Or it could be said, when people are looking they are not seeing. Looking is not seeing.

If I knew everything I would not need to have faith. People who think they know everything or if they can't intellectually comprehend or explain the existence of God have little need for faith. Believing that there is something beyond human comprehension is called faith.

> *" 'Faith' is not an affirmation of a creed, an intellectual acceptance of God, or believing certain doctrines to be true or orthodox (although those things might well be good). Such intellectual assent does not usually change your heart or your lifestyle. I'm convinced that much modern atheism is a result of such a heady and really ineffective definition of faith. Both Jesus' and Paul's notion of faith is much better translated as foundational confidence or trust that God cares about what is happening right now. This is clearly the quality that Jesus fully represents and then praises in other people.*
> *God refuses to be known intellectually. God can only be loved and known in the act of love; God can only be experienced in communion. This is why Jesus "commands" us to move toward love and fully abide there. Love is like a living organism, an active force-field upon which we can rely, from which we can draw, and which we can allow to pass through us. I am afraid you can believe doctrines (e.g., virgin birth, biblical inerrancy, Real Presence in bread and wine, etc.) to be true and not enjoy such a radical confidence in love or God at all."*
>
> Richard Rohr

◆ *Do you have or have you had important religious experiences?*

When asked if I have had an important religious experience, the first thought that comes to mind is the phenomena of a vision or having the experience of my Rosary turning to gold. I heard about such things happening but none has happened to me. I have an open mind and don't deny such things are happening, just not to me.

Maybe this is not what the question is asking. Intensive journaling can be an important spiritual experience. An example is recorded earlier in this book in the journaling with my parents.

Comparing my journaling with my deceased mother, a dialogue is going on and I am so touched by it that it brings tears to my eyes each time I read it. It seems so real, as if we are sitting next to each other on a love seat. With Dad, it is so different. There was no dialogue, full of criticism and guilt. In my heart of hearts I know my father loved me very much and I love him also. There is obviously something psychological going on in the journaling. My point is intensive journaling can be an important spiritual experience.

I can relate to what a priest said at a funeral I attended. He said, "I have news for you, we all are going to die and the question is, what are you doing to prepare for it?" Going to a funeral of a loved one can be a religious experience for me. We all know that our death is part of the journey, but what am I doing to prepare for that event? I can answer that question by saying that writing this book is a way of searching for a deeper meaning of the real me.

Contemplation of my traits, temperament, a life lived, is where my religious or spiritual experience is. Not to forget the significance of answering these penetrating life questions. All can be a true growth experience. The priest was right about preparing for the event of death. Getting to know the real me is a way to prepare for our death and formulate a positive worldview.

◆ *What feelings do you have when you think about God?*

I read somewhere that God should not be thought of as responsible for everything. Instead, that God is everything.

> *"The very energy, the very intelligence, the very elegance and passion that make it all go. That deep emotional conviction of the presence of a superior reasoning power, which is revealed in the incomprehensible universe, forms my idea of God."*
>
> Albert Einstein

My vision of God is not a figure sitting on a throne in the sky. God can be found and lives in our soul. God can't be found by adding anything, but is found by subtracting stuff from my false self that is alive and lives in my head, not my heart.

I think of God as the core energy of all unconditional love in the universe. A love that is boundless. A continuous energy that is inclusive, not exclusive, and that God is alive and is the present energy in every living thing on the planet.

> *"Our idea of God tells us more about ourselves than about Him."*
>
> Thomas Merton

There is a lot to think about in that sentence. Our weakness is a euphemism I call *"falling off the wagon."* When I fall off the wagon, I trust God's grace as always there forgiving, a boundless grace. I also know this forgiveness doesn't mean I don't have a responsibility to try to do my best. I think this boundless energy of love is what God wants all of us strive for, to love unconditionally. To be unknown by God is just too much privacy.

> *"As I grow older, faith for me has become a daily readiness to allow and to trust the force field, knowing that it is good, that it's totally on my side, and that I'm already inside of it. How else can I really be at peace?"*
>
> Author unknown

◆ *Do you consider yourself a religious person?*

Yes, I do feel I am a religious person. As I discussed in an earlier question, "What can you tell me about your religion and faith?" I see religion and faith not really the same but partners in my journey.

◆ *If you pray, what do you feel is going on when you pray?*

I do pray, but my prayer life has changed over the years from the recitation of prayers to more contemplative prayer.

> *"What is the use of praying if at the very moment of prayer, we have so little confidence in God that we are busy planning our own kind of answer to our prayer?"*
>
> Thomas Merton

Prayer for me is now more contemplative as Father Rohr describes: *"Prayer, which has become a functional and pious thing for believers to do, was meant to be a descriptor and an invitation to inner experience. When spiritual teachers invite you to "pray," they are in effect saying, "Go inside and know for yourself!"*

Some recitation of prayer can lead me to contemplative prayer, an inner experience.

Whether my prayer life is one of contemplation or of recitation, the purpose is the same. To grow closer to God and to ask for the strength to deal with whatever cards are dealt to me in life. To have a positive attitude and courage to stay the course, not to lose faith. Here are a couple prayers on my recitation list. This prayer was written by Thomas Merton, found in his book *Thoughts in Solitude.*

"My Lord God, I have no idea where I am going. I do not see the road ahead of me. I cannot know for certain where it will all end. Nor do I really know myself, and the fact that I think that I am following your will does not mean that I am actually doing so. But I believe that the desire to please you does in fact please you, and I hope I have that desire in all that I am doing. I hope that I will

never do anything apart from that desire. I know that if I do this you will lead me by the right road though I may know nothing about it. Therefore, I will trust you always though I may seem to be lost and in the shadow of death. I will not fear, for you are ever with me, and you will never leave me to face my perils alone."

Recitation of this prayer is an inner experience, speaking to my need for humility and trust. About conviction and faith, knowing that God is always with me. The recognition that I am not in control.

Prayer is not mumbling words while your mind is on what others are doing. At meal time or anytime else. Allowing our heart and mind to be changed is what's going on in prayer. Too many times prayer becomes a habit, not words of gratitude or petition.

Recitation of passages from the Bible can be prayer for me. The following is an example.

Romans 5: 3-5: *"We can rejoice, too, when we run into problems and trials for we know that they are good for us—they help us learn to be patient. And patience develops strength of character in us and helps us trust God more each time we use it until finally our hope and faith are strong and steady. Then, when that happens, we are able to hold our heads high no matter what happens and know that all is well, for we know how dearly God loves us, and we feel this warm love everywhere within us because God has given us the Holy Spirit to fill our hearts with his love."*

Kathleen Dowling book *The Grace in Dying* wrote about *dual thinking.* Being judgmental with thoughts like, how will I look if I do this or what's in it for me? It is making judgements as to what is good and what is bad.

Non-dual consciousness, or living in the moment, is what the goal should be. Without judging or thinking the present moment or event is good or bad. You are unattached from critique, analysis or outcome. It's without your *ego deciding* whether we like it or not. The non-dual mind is one open to God in prayer.

"The non-dual contemplative mind is a whole new mind for most people! With it, you can stand back and compassionately observe the self or any event from an appropriately detached viewing platform. This is the most immediate and practical meaning of "dying to self" I can think of. As a general rule if you cannot detach from something, you are far too attached to it".

Richard Rohr

The book *Open Mind, Open Heart* by Thomas Keating has led many to a path of contemplative prayer also described as Centering Prayer. He says, *"It is accessed by letting go of our own idea of ourselves, turning our will over to God, and resting in the Divine In dwelling that is already present within us and waiting to reveal itself to us."*

Contemplative prayer is a way for us to work on emotional programing. The ego is reminding us, it wants to be in control. Answering and reflecting on these penetrating questions is a form of prayer. My prayer life will be showing growth when I can say, *prayer happened today instead of, I prayed today.*

We should let go of personal agendas and expectations. It is entering *our inner room* to find detachment from our habitual faults and thinking patterns that seem to be stored in our brain. They tend to reactivate every time a situation pushes the appropriate button that tells our head to lose control.

◆ ***Do you feel that your religious outlook is "true?" In what sense?***

I think my religious outlook is right for me, but not necessarily for others. I have heard many times "religion is not a spectator sport." Religion is about community and participation, where I can feel the love of others. There are many paths for each of us to find that community. I do think that the idea of community can get lost in the idea of belonging to an institution. Maybe this is why some do not connect religion with community. There are different principles embraced by religious communities and it doesn't mean one is all right or one is all wrong. I think they all can lead to a path of spiritually bringing you closer to God. We are each led by the Holy Spirit in choosing our path.

Doing for others as we would have others do unto us, is a core principle we all can embrace. All of us are part of the larger part. We are all connected, including the earth we live on. Because of this connection, when we do good for others, we are really doing good to ourselves.

◆ *Are religious traditions other than your own "true?"*

The following is from Daily meditations, Center for Contemplation: Father Rohr and Jim Finley: *"Salvation" has little to do with belief systems, belonging to the right group, or correct ritual practice. It has everything to do with living right here, right now, and knowing a beautiful and fully accepting God is this very moment given to you.*". The message is —the messages are all far bigger than any single religion.

The "Christ Mystery" is much bigger than Christianity as an organized religion. If we don't understand this, Christians will have little ability to make friends with, build bridges to, understand, or respect other religions or the planet. Jesus did not come to create a country club or a tribe of people who could say, "We're in and you're out. We've got the truth and you don't."

◆ *What is sin (sins)? How have your feelings about this changed (as a child, an adolescent and so on)?*

In his book *Falling Upward*, Richard Rohr talks about the two halves of life. That we each are given a span of years to discover our true self. The first part of our life is to build *a container or identity, and the second is to discover what the contents of that the container was meant to hold.*

During the first half of my life the meaning of sin was formed by what I was told in the family structure that developed boundaries and self-worth as my identity was being developed. If you were a good boy you received a reward. If you were a bad boy you were punished.

I love a comment made at George H. W. Bush's celebration of life by Allan Simpson. Paraphrased, *"Hate erodes the container from within where it lives."*

In the second half of my life sin was defined by how I loved, by what I should hold, and what I should let go. Going to confession is a good way to define my view of the difference between a youth's idea of sin compared to an adult understanding. As an adolescent going to confession could be the confession of conduct in the past, confessing what I was told is wrong. Those actions frankly were over at that point. [over doesn't make them right] An adult going to confession is to make a commitment of transformation for the future. It is not about what I did, but what I am going to do, that is forward thinking. What I should let go of, that is a mature approach to defining sin. It defines what is meant to be held in my container during the second half of life. Merton said, *"I minimize my own sins and compensate for doing so by exaggerating the faults of others."* [I need to stay on guard and aware of my actions]

I have moved beyond doctrines and dogmas. I have adopted more of a Bonaventure Theology, we all are one, not fear based, it is all about love. Not a stick and carrot philosophy receiving the prize for following the rules. Father Rohr said *"Authentic spirituality is always first about you—about allowing your own heart and mind to be changed. It's about getting your own who right. Who is it that is doing the perceiving? Is it your illusory, separate, false self; or is it your True Self, who you are."*

Looking to the future is one reason I feel the Enneagram can be a good tool to identify what sin is for me. Identifying my strengths and weaknesses [my traits on the Enneagram] examining the way I answer penetrating questions gives me insight to see my weaknesses [sin], my shadow side, and what I deny. Identification of my weaknesses gives me an opportunity to transform those actions of my false self that lives in the head and transform us to our true self, in my heart where God lives.

◆ *Some people believe that without religion morality breaks down. What do you think?*

For centuries morality and religion have been bedfellows. The evolution of thought defining morality and defining religion is another issue. What was considered moral when I was a child is far from today's definition.

Much of today's religious instruction has various value frameworks as to what is right and wrong. Religion and morality are not as synonymous as it was in centuries past. Some people today describe themselves as not religious but spiritual. I know atheists who are very moral and respectful of others. So yes, it is possible.

I see the current evolution for the religious communities challenged with the growth of our secular society. Change is hard for large institutions to implement, but change is needed.

> *"When the bullseye becomes as big as an elephant in your mind, you won't be able to miss it."*
>
> Alejandro Jodorows

I am not sure our religious leaders see the elephant in the room.

◆ *Where do you feel that you are changing, growing, struggling or wrestling with doubt in your life at the present time? Where is your growing edge?*

At this writing, I am 81 years old and 25 years since I started living with cancer, I have been growing, struggling with doubt in my life. To that point, 25 years ago, I had it *"my way"* with accomplishing professional goals set, personal desires met, and family well along with their lives and doing well; life was good. A life changing event when being told the present statistics give you 3 to 4 years of life gets your attention. Statistics can be like a person drowning in a river with an average depth of 2 feet. By the Grace of God, good meds, and several operations, God has given me a lot more time to get it right.

Working on humility is the key to getting closer to God. I know that it is not about being correct but being connected. Easier said than done. Yes, that is a struggle. Somewhere along the way I got the message that I'm not in control. My body isn't either. My life is part of a much bigger mystery and it is in the hands of something far greater than me.

I recently read on Facebook the following "The Native American Code of Ethics." These questions are where does my growing edge reside, this is what love is all about and the more of this code we can adopt, the more we can be on our cutting edge to accomplish what God has put us on this earth to learn.

1. **Rise with the sun to pray.** Pray alone. Pray often. The Great Spirit will listen, if you only speak.

2. **Be tolerant of those who are lost on their Path.** Ignorance, conceit, anger, jealousy and greed stem from a lost soul. Pray that they will find guidance.

3. **Search for yourself, by yourself.** Do not allow others to make your path for you. It is your road, and yours alone. Others may walk it with you, but no one can walk it for you.

4. **Treat the guests in your home with much consideration.**

Serve them the best food, give them the best bed and treat them with respect and honor.

5. **Do not take what is not yours whether from a person, a community, the wilderness or from a culture.** It was not earned nor given. It is not yours.

6. **Respect all things that are placed upon this earth** – whether it be people, animals or plant.

7. **Honor other people's thoughts, wishes and words.** Never interrupt another or mock or rudely mimic them. Allow each person the right to personal expression.

8. **Never speak of others in a bad way.** The negative energy that you put out into the universe will multiply when it returns to you.

9. **All persons make mistakes.** And all mistakes can be forgiven.

10. **Bad thoughts cause illness of the mind, body and spirit.** Practice optimism.

11. **Nature is not FOR us, it is a PART of us.** Animals, plants and other living creatures are all part of your worldly family.

12. **Children are the seeds of our future.** Plant love in their hearts and water them with wisdom and life's lessons. When they are grown, give them space to grow.

13. **Avoid hurting the hearts of others.** The poison of your pain will return to you.

14. **Be truthful at all times.** Honesty is the test of one's will within this universe.

15. **Keep yourself balanced.** Your Mental self, Spiritual self, Emotional self, and Physical self need to be strong, pure and healthy. Work out the body to strengthen the mind. Grow rich in spirit to cure emotional ails.

16. **Make conscious decisions as to who you will be and how you will react.** Be responsible for your own actions.

17. **Respect the privacy and personal space of others.** Do not touch the personal property of others – especially sacred and religious objects. This is forbidden.

18. **Be true to yourself first.** You cannot nurture and help others if you cannot nurture and help yourself first.

19. **Respect others' religious beliefs.** Do not force your belief on others.

20. **Share your good fortune with others.** Participate in charity.

We may differ in our faith, religion, and culture, yet we all live together on the same boat. We are only custodians and not owners of the earth, not to be its conquerors nor its destroyers. Nothing goes away, everything goes somewhere.

Remember the 5 R'S—**Reduce, Refuse, Reuse, Recycle, Remove.**

◆ *What is your image of mature faith?*

About 20 years ago while reflecting on my life's purpose this question did come to my mind along with rethinking spiritual values. I now see the groups and institutions to which I belonged to from a more objective viewpoint. I do appreciate their value but no longer see them only as divine but rather as human inventions to help us on our journey of faith.

I think it is easy not to move on, to grow, to transform your life to what you may call the "further journey." Without study, prayer, and commitment it is easy to get stuck in trench thinking that it is all about learning to obey the rules and those who obey them win the prize.

Somewhere along our journey of life, we have to stop and ask ourselves, what does it mean and why am I doing this or that? I feel a mature faith is a commitment of one's life to God. This ultimately must be determined by one's conscience. It is about moving thoughts to the heart.

We were created by God to share his love in the world. Taking our first breath was with God's blessing. Our life started with innocence. Our experiences during life cause us to lose track of our real self. A commitment to a mature faith is to practice spiritual disciplines to get rid of illusions so that we can see what is, see who we are, and see what is happening. Recognizing that God is alive within us.

"The more we empty ourselves, the more room we give God to fill us."
St. Mother Teresa

Mature faith is living your faith every day of the week!

Part V:
Your Life Story

Youth is the best time to be rich,
and the best time to be poor. ...

Writing Your Story

Our environment, the one we are born into, we will carry the stones from this foundation in our backpack for our entire life. It is in those special moments, the trials, failures, and choices that we make is when we grow. Our life story reveals our temperament and traits. Offering insights and growth opportunities.

"We are what we see. We are products of our surroundings."
Amber Valletta

Your temperament, traits and the dialogue you have with the penetrating questions make up the fertile ground of your life story. In writing your story, review your entries and notes that reflect your temperament and traits. It is important that we dialogue with the penetrating questions. Some of us don't want to go there. The questions are probing places we are wanting to avoid. Your dialogue with them will reflect wisdom and choices made in your life. A beacon of light on the true self.

Look for how your life story may differ from others. How different was the environmental and geographic area of formative years from a Nebraska farm boy?

In writing my story my temperament and traits did shine a light on the real me. They disclosed abundant growth opportunities for me. You will discover the same while writing your story. Your story is interesting when it relates to the lives of the reader and people you know and love. Especially those people who lived in a similar environment. My story may be helpful in writing yours if it reminds you of those you know or events and relationships in your life. You will be able to see my temperament, traits, and my dialogue with the questions as they surface in my story. You will see the same in yours.

"Don't become a mere recorder of facts, but try to penetrate the mystery of their origin."

Ivan Pavlov

If you have read my book *Dialogue with My Soul* you have read my story before. *Dialogue with My Soul* captured my youth, high school days, Navy experiences, career, detailing every move and promotion, cars owned, pets loved and vacations took. This type of story is of interest to our children and grandchildren. They want to know about vacations and cars you drove, and see lots of photos. It is important for your story not to just include the facts and events, but share insights to the choices you made in your life. The MBTI, The Enneagram, and the penetrating questions is where you find the good soil to cultivate, grow and develop those stories about your choices made in life.

An autobiography can be facts of an entire life, but your story should be one about a life lived. Our story should paint a picture of our values, beliefs, choices made, and commitments for our remaining days. This thread is the origin of the fabric weaving our life.

"Life is not about making a name for yourself but uncovering the name you always had."

Richard Rohr

We all have a great story to tell. To share your life story is one of the building blocks to *transforming your worldview and finding your true self*. Our stories are deepened by our experiences and relationships.

Being 81 years old I carry more wisdom, baggage and blessings than a 25 year old person. My dialogue is not the same, being blessed with a full life. Reflecting on our past relationships, losses, crises, suffering and blessings can be healing and gratifying. If you are 25 years old your story may include more hopes and goals for the future. Your journal can be a wealth of information. If you don't journal now you may want to consider doing so.

Thoughts to consider in writing your story:

- My life story may trigger some thoughts for your story.
- James Fowler's book *Faith Stages* has a great outline to follow in writing your story.
- What do you hope to accomplish in the future?
- What effect has failure or regret had on your life?
- Social issues or causes about which you are passionate about?
- How did your fundamental beliefs and values develop?
- How have you coped with major health problem, challenge, or crisis?
- Are there challenges, struggles encountered in your life?

My Story
Reflection of Childhood Memories

It was December 24,1937. I was born on the same farm where my father was born on November 20, 1900. I was delivered at home by a family doctor who practiced medicine in a small village of 600 residents 6 miles from home. In the lottery of life, none of us have a choice of choosing the circumstances and environment of our birth.

Growing up on a farm in the Midwest 81 years ago was different from growing up in a city, or on a farm today. The farm life of the 1940's was self-sustaining where we produced most of our food. We had pigs, chickens, cows and raised grain and hay for the animals. The grain that was not used for the livestock was sold. Milk that was not used was separated, skim milk from the cream. The cream was sold to a creamery in town and the skim milk was fed to the pigs.

My parents butchered the animals for the pork, chicken and beef that we ate. They made sausages, cured and canned the meat as we had little refrigeration. From the rendering of the meat, my mother made soap to wash our clothes. Flour to bake the bread came in cloth sacks with different patterns on the cloth flour sacks. My mother made shirts for me from those flour sacks. Our meals were cooked on a wood burning cookstove.

The fuel we used for the cookstove was cobs from the corn we grew in the fields. We had running water in the house, but no bathroom. Baths were taken in a washtub. The house was heated by an oil heating stove on the first floor. The second floor where the bedrooms were had no heat, with the exception of some heat rising through a floor register in one room.

The closest farm to ours was 1/2 mile away and there were no other children close by to play with. My brother was 6 years older and my sister 10 years older than me. Being the youngest I did get a lot of attention from my elder siblings. I remember playing in the dirt and pretending that I was in the field like dad plowing the field or

cultivating the crops. I would ride our pony and wander about the farm and country roads pretending I was a cowboy. I had a lot of time to myself and a lot of time to daydream. I loved the farm and the time I had to ride my pony, and the time I had to daydream.

I loved the horses and before I could ride by myself Dad sometimes would give me a ride on one of the work horses after a day's work in the field on their way to the barn. We always had a pony and I learned to ride a horse bare back at a young age. My parents would not let me learn to ride with a saddle, because they feared if I fell off the horse, and my foot caught in the stirrup of the saddle, I could be dragged by the horse. I would lead the horse next to a wagon, climb on the wagon so I could mount the horse. While I was learning, I sometimes would get as far as a half mile from the wagon and fall off. I would then lead the horse back to the wagon to get back on the horse. It turned out to be a good incentive to learn not to fall off the horse. I guess from an early age I was very persistent.

Lessons of Responsibility

There was always an expectation of being responsible in my family. My responsibilities of gathering eggs from the chicken house and cobs from the corn crib for the cook stove were expanded to helping with other chores. I didn't have any younger brothers or sisters, so I still had to get the cobs for the cook stove, but I think Mom helped out gathering the eggs. As responsibilities increased, I was feeding livestock, getting the milk cows from the pasture, and then milking the cows. My parents gave me livestock to raise as my own. Caring for them and sending them to market provided me spending money and taught me how to save part of the money I earned.

With work to be done on the farm there wasn't much time for play. Work took priority over any sports. Dad never had a chance to play any sports as a child; however, Mom did try to play some with me when she had time. The bottom line is there was work to be done and I didn't have time to play sports. I never developed the skill or confidence to participate in sports at school.

While plowing the fields I wondered about how my life would have been different if I was born in India, France, or maybe New York City. Growing up on the plains of Nebraska as a young person, I had a lot of time to daydream while I was riding my horse or plowing. The field had half-mile long rows, so when driving the tractor, having only to concentrate on keeping the tractor going straight down the furrow gave me a lot of time to daydream.

Formation of Religious/Social Values

Through my teenage years, I grew up in a family where I was expected to go to church on Sunday. Our church, St. John Lutheran, was in Beatrice, Nebraska about 12 miles from the farm. We had to travel for about 2 miles of the trip on a dirt road, before we reached a gravel road to Beatrice. Dad removed the fenders on our 1928 Pontiac, so when it rained the mud wouldn't bawl up under the fenders of the car. By the time we reached Beatrice, mud was everywhere on the car. Dad always stopped at a service station and washed the car off so we didn't get dirty getting out of the car for church.

At church I had time to socialize with other children in events such as the Christmas pageant. I normally played the part of a shepherd boy or one of the wise men. I never landed the part of Joseph. After the pageant all the children received a sack with candy and an orange as a gift.

A Christmas gift I remember receiving as a child at home was a holster for my toy gun and chaps my mother made for me from an old sheep skin coat my dad had worn. Another gift I remember was a pair of cowboy boots that I wanted so badly. After I got them they did not fit right and they hurt my feet, so I never wore them much. I think that disappointed my parents because they were expensive to purchase.

On rainy days there was not much work to do on the farm so we would go to town to shop or go to a movie. We enjoyed going to western movies with Hop-a-long Cassidy, Gene Autry or Roy Rogers. My parents liked to sit in the car on main street and watch the people. They would let my brother and I wander around town. We would like to go to the 5 and 10 cent store in town to look at the toys on sale. Our telephone at home was on a party line and our ring was two longs and one short. When it was time to go home, my parents would blow the car horn two longs and one short. When we heard the horn we knew it was time to head home.

The world is inclusive as we all are one, different cultures, environments, and the stories about our lives tells how our upbringing is only a part of a substantially broader story unfolding in America.

Our country painted a different landscape of good fortune during my youth, and active years, different than for millennials today.

It was my time in the history of our country when:

- It was a common goal for most people to seek employment with a company that could provide potential growth for your talents with the idea that you will retire from that company after 30 years of service.

- I lived in a time when the American dream of family and home embraced stability. Neighbors looked out for one another, property was clean and tidy, and most families attended religious services regularly. Today, less than half of young people say they attend religious services weekly and about one-fifth say they never attend religious services.

- I enjoyed TV shows like *The Phil Silvers Show*, *The Adventures of Ozzie and Harriet*, *Father Knows Best*, and *Leave it To Beaver* that shared a message different from today's reality shows. We got our first TV when I was 15 years old.

- I grew up in the period after World War II when our country experienced one of the greatest upgrades to our standard of living.

- Many young men returning from World War II went to college on the GI Bill; many of them being the first in their family to attend college.

- Our parents—to their dying day—carried the thrift mentality scars from the Depression. Our generation became the one willing to take on debt. Credit cards and other methods of personal financing became "the way" to purchase cars, appliances and anything that improved our standard of living. By 1970, for the first time in the history of the U.S., more than half the families held a credit card.

These examples of unfolding events in American life during my upbringing had an effect on everyone's lifestyle. There was a sense of responsibility and hope in pursuing a better life. There was high regard of the self-made person. But—where you lived did make a difference. The landscape between urban and rural American life at the time of our upbringing contributed to dramatic differences— New York City and a Nebraska farm were vastly different.

Today's communication and technology has bridged many of these differences. Cultural backgrounds and environments contributed to choices families made while I was growing up. The small family farm I lived on has all but disappeared.

When and where I was born was not a choice. Ultimately as we become adults it is our responsibility to choose. It is all about choices, isn't it?

Sharing Values with a Friend

When I was writing my book, "*A Dialogue with My Soul,*" I called Bill Cassidy on the phone and asked him if he would read my manuscript and consider sharing some of the stories and events of his life while growing up in New York. I was delighted when he agreed to share the stories of his family and his life. Bill and I worked together for a number of years at Kodak and always had a great relationship. It is clear our backgrounds are very different—but an interesting discovery for me was that our core values are very similar, which I think is important and significant.

The following is Bill's response:

My initial reaction in reading your manuscript, "A Dialogue with My Soul" was a flood of thoughts that include these:

- *Two men from dramatically different backgrounds and environments actually share a common thread of values, purpose, spiritual, and desire to excel that was a reflection of our parents and a nurturing but challenging upbringing.*
- *We share a common journey that has been one of continuing education and growth with a current focus on deeper reflection and assessment of what is the most meaningful manner to live our final years.*
- *A recognition that the ultimate priorities, time and effort must be directed at: unconditional love of our family and friends.*
- *Applying ourselves to never lose sight of our life's purpose and goal—Salvation.*
- *A painful awareness that I really know very little about the historical roots of my parents, grandparents, and ancestors.*

Bill's input meant that *life is about* the foundational blocks that we acquire during our formative years are not tied to when or where we live. Our worldview is tied to values, purpose, and spiritual awareness. As Bill stated, *"applying ourselves to never lose sight of our life's purpose and goal—Salvation."*

Include Some Human Interest Stories

I started driving the tractor that Dad got around 1944 and started doing field work about the age of 10; plowed the fields and cultivated the crops. This was during the summer months when school was not in session. I will always remember one day when Dad stopped by to see how I was getting along. I told him that I heard they were giving swimming lessons in town at the YMCA and I would like to be able to take the lessons. I can still see him so clearly looking to the north and then the south and then the east and then to the west. No matter what direction you would look you could see nothing but the flat plains of Nebraska. Most days you could see for 12 miles.

His response to my request was, "Where are you going to drown?" He made his point, and I did not have a better answer. I got back on the tractor and continued plowing the field for the next crop. I later learned to swim when I joined the Navy.

Turning Points

Upon graduation from high school, I joined the Navy, my introduction to the world. Coming from a farming community in Nebraska, 6 miles from a village of 600, 12 miles from a town of 12,000 sheltered me from the real world. I had only been exposed to three African American families. Two were barbers who lived in Beatrice. I thought one of the barbers was brilliant. When he cut my hair, he knew all my relatives, my birthday, and my relatives' birthdays also. Maybe he just kept good notes, but I was impressed.

In the Navy I was assigned to an aircraft carrier living in a compartment with about 30 young men of various cultures including some African Americans. Their homes were from all over: Los Angeles, Wisconsin and "the city" [I learned that the city is not Omaha but New York City]. We were all radiomen working, sleeping, and eating together. On liberty in Norfolk, when I boarded the ferry to Newport News, I discovered an African American was not allowed to pee next to me or drink out of the same water fountain. What is this all about? Welcome to the world, farm boy.

I was one month short of being 20 years old when Monica and I married in 1957. Then it was not unusual for people to marry at the age of 21, but 19 was very young to make a commitment for life. Monica and I have been married 60 plus years and I have worked my way up to an annual contract renewal with Monica from a daily commitment: "you better straighten up buddy." Life is good.

Home on leave with my nephew Kenny

Two DeWitt Youths Enlist in U.S. Navy

Two DeWitt youths, Donald C. Wollenberg, son of Mr. and Mrs. Otto E. Wollenberg, and Roger E. Mahloch, son of Mr. and Mrs. August Mahloch, have enlisted in

Mahloch   Wollenberg

the Navy through the Beatrice recruiting station.

Both have been sent to the Great Lakes Naval Training Center for nine weeks of recruit training. Mahloch will attend a trade school in the field of electronics after completion of recruit training.

USS Valley Forge CVS-45

Monica in our two room apartment

After our wedding in Nebraska we returned to Norfolk with all our belongings in the car. My sailor's pay was very modest. Monica immediately was hired for a position in the accounting department of a bank to supplement our income. Our apartment consisted of a bedroom, kitchen and a shared bath, for $75 a month. Later we moved to an apartment with a bedroom, living room, kitchen and a bath.

Long lasting marriages today just aren't as common as back when we married. Today approximately 50% of marriages end in divorce. Also, when Monica and I married, marriage in American society for the most part had clearly defined gender roles. The husband traditionally held the role of the breadwinner; the wife lived the role of caregiver. Through the years the traditional gender roles have changed and it is not uncommon to see them reversed today. The roles in our relationship have been modified over the years due to many circumstances and needs at the time—but they haven't changed all that much. At times Monica has played both roles of breadwinner and caregiver.

The role we play is not as important as the commitment and respect we have for each other. Our marriage did not endure without mistakes, bruised feelings, and many difficult challenges along the way. We have had many good times and certainly some disagreements and bad times. We worked through the trials as they came, and more trials will come along. Disappointments and pain result in a stronger bond between us. We have worked together with a commitment and resolve to our relationship. No one person has all the right answers and we chose to integrate not compromise, in making decisions best for our relationship.

It is not my money or your money, it is our money. It is not my car or your car. I open the mail and Monica pays the bills and the list can go on. I am not suggesting our way is the right way, but to demonstrate what works for us and our attitude is that stuff is not as important as the quality of time we spend together.

> *"There are three ways of dealing with difference: domination, compromise, and integration. By domination only one side gets what it wants; by compromise neither side gets what it wants; by integration we find a way by which both sides may get what they wish."*
>
> Mary Parker Follett

Monica has always contributed to financial need of our marriage. When I was discharged from the Navy and we headed back to Nebraska she obtained a position at the Nebraska State Legislature. When our children were born she took on the role of caregiver, and continued to work part-time outside the home keeping books for a drug store close to our house. After the children were in middle school she started a 15 year career with Kodak. When I decided to become a realtor Monica also obtained her real estate license with me, and we worked together in the real estate business.

The older we get the more we realize time is our most important asset. To love each other as we are, embracing the idea that we can't or don't want to change each other. With time it becomes clear that it is not what each person gets out of our relationship but what each can give. Our love for each

other has evolved into a relationship different than what is promoted by the mass media. We feel so very fortunate that God brought us together! It would be hard to imagine life otherwise without our deep love and commitment to each other.

Children Grow Up Fast, Enjoy Them

As our children were growing up, letting them play outside and do their own thing was common. We let them walk to school which was within a reasonable distance. It was less distance than the distance my dad told me he walked to school from his farm home, three miles in snow to his knees, and of course, uphill both ways.

Because of safety issues, today's children are not left unsupervised to play outside. Sports are more organized and very competitive. Every child (or their parents) wants them to play in the NFL or NBA.

We are proud of both of our children and what they have accomplished with their lives. Beth has been married to Paul over 30 years. Beth has always been a giving person. To her students while being a teacher, as an administrative person, owning her own

Beth & Paul
October 18, 1986

Tim & Rowena
April 7, 1990

business, and a stay at home mom, she has demonstrated her gift of caring and giving for others over and over again. Both Paul and Beth share responsibilities, make sacrifices and choices to support their children, Joe and Natalie. Their example is one of unconditional love.

Tim and Rowena have been married 28 plus years and both have chosen a career of service to others. Tim is a medical doctor [radiologist] and Rowena, who is educated as an attorney, actively volunteers in their community using her gifts helping others.

An article I read from—*BBC mobile news report [education and family]* peeked my interest as my eyes took notice of the headline, *"1970s and 1980s were the best time to raise children."* Then under this heading was raised the question: They may have been better for the parents, but were they better bringing up children during that period of time?

Every generation reflects on their childhood and wants to provide for their children the opportunities that they missed growing up. As with all things in life, balance seems to be the fundamental principle that most people strive to attain. If the parent was deprived of material goods as a child, they are inclined to give their children more.

For the parent with material wealth, they struggle with what is the right balance of stuff to give the children. How do we instill the values of responsibility, honesty, respect that inspires motivation for the child to always do their best, and make good choices? The simple answer is by example. But it is not that simple and there is much more to consider including the environment and culture lived at the time.

For me, sometimes letting go was painful and maybe it was because I felt a loss of control. I cried the day we let our son out of our car starting his freshman year at college. He was our youngest and it was at that moment I realized our youngest child was starting a new phase of his life and we too were starting a new phase of ours. It was a time when I reflected that I was glad we took the family vacations we took, that we made it a practice to have family meals together, and thankful for all those wonderful memories we made together.

I've made mistakes parenting in words and deeds that I regret and have apologized for those I know about. For mistakes I don't know that I probably made I am sorry. Focus on my career, not finding a proper balance did leave me with regrets. Every time I hear the song, "Cat's in the Cradle" by Harry Chapin, it rings loud in my ear. I wish I would have spent more time with our children.

A lot going on here.

Finding My Way in the Work World

The years 1959 through 1962 were ones of adjustment and searching for a direction in my life. I always wanted to be a farmer, but during the years in the Navy my brother married and entered into a joint venture of farming with my father. Dad did not have enough land or the probability to rent enough additional land that would support my brother and me in a farming operation. Joining the family farming operation was not an option.

I was discharged from the Navy early in December 1958. I went to the employment office to look for temporary work before the Holidays. When I filled out the application, they noticed my experience as a radioman in the Navy. I was told about a position available at the Nebraska Highway Patrol as a radio dispatcher.

The position required copying Morse code. Communications between state police departments state to state was by Morse code. Communications with the troopers on the road, however, was voice. The position paid $325 per month and after discussing it with Monica, we decided it would be in our best interest for me to apply for the position as this opportunity would provide employment for me in an area where I had experience.

We had planned to move to Colorado, but if we moved to Colorado, our prospect for employment was unknown. Monica had worked for the state in Lincoln before we were married and was confident she could acquire another position at the state capitol if I got the job with the Highway Patrol. I applied for the position and was hired and soon after we moved to Lincoln, Monica got a position at the state. The proceedings during the legislative session were recorded by a stenographer and Monica filled that position.

My position with the Highway Patrol required a communications license. Part of the test to obtain the license required copying Morse code, 16 words a minute with a pencil. In the Navy I learned the Morse code and keyboarding at the same time. When I heard the sound of a character, my fingers would unconsciously go to the proper key of the typewriter. I was performing well on the job and copying Morse code at 30 words a minute on the typewriter.

I went to Kansas City to take the test after several months on the job; I failed the test. I had three mistakes in five minutes of testing and the requirement was to copy five minutes of Morse code with no mistakes. It was compulsory to copy the code using a pencil. This required me to concentrate on the character before I put it on the test paper with the pencil. I was fired from my job.

While I was in the Navy and my ship was in dry dock, I was sent on a brief assignment to a shore communications center. The position at the communications center was not challenging and I had a lot of time off. I decided I would get a part time job to fill the time.

I responded to an ad in the paper, "Manager wants part time help to promote a product." I did not have a clue what the job was about, but I applied and was hired to sell encyclopedias door-to-door. The manager gave me a script with a sales pitch and I memorized it verbatim. I sold three sets the first night on the job.

Waking Up at 5 AM to Deliver Ice Cream

It was the sales success I experienced selling encyclopedias that made me respond to the following ad. *Fairmont Foods Company "Wants route salesman starting at $375 per month."* I did not have a clue what a route salesman did, but I knew that $375 dollars a month was $50 more a month than the job I was just fired from.

I was hired for the job. The job turned out to be selling and delivering ice cream to stores, stocking the display cases. I also delivered ice cream to lunch counters. Five days a week my day started at 5 AM, and most days ended at 6 PM. I loaded the truck myself each day. The truck needed defrosting every few weeks. This was done on Wednesdays, my day off. It was a very physical job convincing me to look for another job.

The first check was for more than $400. I was paid a base salary [$375] plus a commission based on the volume of ice cream sold. I observed that the best place for ice cream was in the display case. The consumer often would choose ice cream from the center of the case, unless they had a preference for a specific brand.

Building good relationships with grocers was key to getting prime merchandising spots in the display cases. Building and maintaining good rapport with others is a core value I learned from my parents. It turned out to be a key factor in much of my good fortune. My good relationship with the grocers was a result of respect for their needs and the needs of their customers. To be on time and not late with deliveries, and to take care and pride in the stocking of my product in the display case.

I enjoyed being with my customers and had a sincere interest in their needs. Until recent years, I got Christmas cards and letters from some of my grocer customer/friends. It was not long before my checks were more than $500 a month and sometimes as high as $600, more money than I could make anywhere else at the time. The money made me change my mind about leaving.

I decided to continue working as a route salesman. Unfortunately, the job was so physical many route salesmen after the age of 40 were burned out. I knew I wanted to do something else, but I was not sure what direction to take. An incident happened that motivated me to make a change.

The Joy of Our First Child's Birth

We had been married for three years before Beth was born. We wanted children and were disappointed as time passed without Monica becoming pregnant. I will always remember the day Monica was coming home from the doctor with the good news. She took the bus to work and had to walk a few blocks from the bus stop to our home. I was sitting on the front porch reading the paper when I saw her approaching our home. It appeared to me she was walking two or three feet off the ground. I knew she had the good news—that she was pregnant.

The day Beth was born, I went to work as always but Monica was starting to have labor pains when I left at 4 AM. I asked her to call me if the time came to go to the hospital. I called her around 8 AM and she asked me to come home. I contacted the office and asked for someone to relieve me on my route. The response to me was, "Do you think Monica would mind taking a cab to the hospital as we do not have anyone here to relieve you?"

Without any response to that comment, I drove the truck to the dairy, left without saying a word to anyone and drove home.

This uncaring response was not a reflection of the company I worked for, but from an employee with poor judgement. Regardless, I made my mind up to move on to another job.

Finding a Rewarding 30 Year Career

My next step was to join Toastmasters and the Junior Chamber of Commerce to network, hoping to find someone who would support me and give me a chance to grow with their company. It was here that I met Jim Eastman who worked for the Eastman Company. [Jim's last name Eastman has no connection with the firm name]

One night at a meeting Jim asked me if I was looking for a change and I said yes. They were looking for a person to service Kodak copy machines. I thought this may be just the opportunity I was looking for.

Jim was well respected by management and his recommendation weighed heavy on the manager's decision. I was hired April 1, 1962, for $102 a week and got a company car. I had reached my goal and this was the start of a very rewarding 30-year career with Eastman Kodak for which I will be ever grateful to Jim Eastman for his unwavering support.

The years 1962 and 1963 were years of transition for our family. It was the start of a promising career with a major corporation. It was also the birth of our second child Timothy, born July 16th 1962. We both wanted to have more children, but it was not to be. We always will be thankful and feel blessed for the gift of our children to share in our lives. Family has always been an important part of our lives.

Learning Corporate Culture

One of my first lessons was becoming part of my new corporate culture. At my first regional meeting in Chicago I was having dinner with my peers one evening. It was a nice restaurant and there were probably six or seven of us at a large round table. Everyone was ordering appetizers, drinks, steaks, lobster, great desserts. After dinner drinks which accompanied the desserts, we got the bill. I remember I ordered chicken, beer, and no dessert. I was conservative with anything that would add to my bill. As was the common practice not known to me, at the end of the meal, the check was split among all at the table. This was the last time I ordered chicken and must admit I love steak and lobster also.

Change is a Part of Corporate Life

Making corporate moves during the 60's through the late 80's was a common practice if you had a goal of advancing within the company. A common mindset was to get a job with a company that provided enough growth for your ability and goals, and stay with that company. It was natural to see employees with 30 years of service to a company. It was unusual to see people move from one company to another. There was loyalty where if you were offered an opportunity to move to a new assignment, you accepted the offer as a step forward with the company. Turning an offer down, in many cases, gave an impression you weren't interested in additional responsibility.

There have always been positive and negative aspects to all corporate careers. On reflection the time you have with your children goes so fast, and I did not grasp how fast until they were gone. I had a constant struggle to find the right balance between family versus career. Those years were informative for our children at the ages 12 and 10 when we moved to Rochester and 17 and 15 when we left. Family was always important but I was always very much focused on my career.

Father Chester Michael, my spiritual director, often told me, *"Roger, keep working on balancing your three P's."* [Power, Pleasure, Possessions]

Being born in 1937 in a modest environment, materialism has

always been a challenge for me. Other colleagues in corporate life at this time came from a similar environment.

Corporate life today is so different. In today's environment loyalty from the employee and from the corporation has changed. No more is it the goal for persons to find one workplace to grow for their entire career. One that your talents would not surpass.

However, there are some things that will never change for those wanting a flourishing career.

Hard work, passion for what you do, determination, [finding a better way] focus on improvements in the task assigned, helping others, networking, learn from mistakes. education, humility and common sense. All education does not come from a book or a degree. It also comes from many of the attributes mentioned. I could go on for pages about specific details in my career that made the difference. One not mentioned that helped me was insecurity. I think it made me work harder.

The following is an outline of my career with Eastman Kodak. Each step along the way I can point to one of the aforementioned attributes that made the difference.

[1962-1967] Sales representative Eastman Kodak Stores, Lincoln, NE.

[1968-1973] Sales representative in St. Louis - supporting dealer salespersons.

[1973] Moved to the corporate offices in Rochester to be an instructor at the Marketing Education Center training salespersons and conducting customer seminars.

[1975] Accepted assignment at corporate headquarters with copy products in customer relations.

[1977] Named coordinator of the customer relations department.

[1978]   A goal of sales management was realized. I was offered a position as sales manager for copy products in Washington, D.C.

[1979]   I was offered the position as a district sales manager in Pittsburgh.

[1983]   I accepted an offer as district manager in Northern Virginia.

[1985]   I was assigned to a corporate executive position. The task was to build relationships with the Civilian Cabinet Secretaries and executives in the agencies, identifying opportunities where the civil cabinet agencies and Kodak could work together.

[1991]   I was offered a position to go to San Paulo, Brazil, to coordinate manufacturing and sales activities for copy products in that country. I accepted the assignment and was excited about the new opportunity. Two weeks after accepting, Kodak announced their first early retirement program. The program for early retirement was not specific to any product line or division. The offer was made company wide to all individuals who were a specific age combined with years of service.

Both Monica and I qualified for the early retirement package; Monica started with Kodak in 1976 with 15 years of service and me with 30 years of service. After examining all the options we decided to not accept the job in San Paulo and we both retired from Eastman Kodak Company in December 1991.

As I think about that time period of my career, I feel fortunate for all the opportunities I had for advancement and being blessed with so much pride and satisfaction professionally and personally. That truly was a long way from scraping cow manure off my shoes before I went to school to a successful career working in the nation's capital. Life was good.

Life after Kodak

I wasn't sure what I wanted to do after leaving Kodak. I enjoyed working for Kodak so if I was going to work for a corporation I would have stayed there. The idea of a totally different work environment appealed to me. I even thought about becoming a blacksmith.

Monica and I took a course in real estate appraising but decided to wait awhile before making a decision to seek employment in that field. We traveled to Japan to visit Paul and Beth, who were in Japan on an assignment with Paul's company. We sold our home in  Fairfax in the spring of 1992 and moved to our Lake Monticello home full time. We purchased a motor home and traveled around the country with our two dogs General Lei and Mai-Tai, with my motorcycle in tow on a trailer behind the motor home. It was in the spring of 1993 that my life was about to embark on a significant change. I was diagnosed with Prostate Cancer.

Change sometimes comes along like an earthquake. Change can be destructive, quite unexpected and painful. Being told at the age of 55 that I had cancer was a shock.

What happened to me was not all that unique; we all experience surprises traveling on our journey of life. Our attitude toward the crisis, is what can affect how the next chapter of our life is going to be. Getting cancer was a wake-up-call. It called to attention the importance of living in the present moment. I took the crisis as a message from God giving me a second chance to get it right—to focus on giving to others and not collecting stuff.

> *"The only things we take with us when we die are the good deeds we have done in charity and love."*
>
> Monsignor Chester Michael

As mentioned earlier in this book, *"You don't see any U-Hauls behind a hearse."* Borrowing words from a Beatles song, "Life is easy with your eyes closed." It is time to open my eyes. Even the most optimistic person at the age of 81 would have to admit that they are now past middle age. People are like snowflakes, all beautiful; but we are all different. I think this is true because we travel on divergent paths to reach this point in our lives as a result of living in a variety of environments.

As a result, each of us has our own unique retrospect on the value of the remaining time allotted to us and choose various ways to spend that time. The choices we make are colored by the emotional, physical, spiritual, and material gifts as well as battles and experiences in our life. Each day it is easier for me to recognize the value of the phrase, "Every day is a gift."

One thing that I feel is constant for me and never changes is— It is not what I experience, but how I react to the experience that makes the difference.

The most important objective for me now is to concentrate on giving joy, love, and peace to others with the time I have left on this earth. It is about my identifying and addressing my faults that can still me from opening my heart to God and to others. As it was shared by my pastor during a recent homily *"it is time for me to tend to the garden of my heart."* The ideal goal would be for me to integrate this attitude into my daily life when relating to others. I still have a lot of work to do, but now is the time for me to make changes by commitment; this is not a time for change by convenience. I have always been a person who likes to have a project to work on. It's is time to work on the project of me. To discover *"The Who I Am."*

"As you spiritually mature, you can forgive your own—and others'— mistakes. You can let go of everyone who hurt you, your former spouse, the boss who fired you, the church, or even God. You have no interest in carrying around negative baggage. Wisdom emerges when you can see everything, you eliminate none of it, and you include all as important training. Finally, everything belongs. You are eventually able to say, from some larger place that may surprise you, "It is what it is" and "even the 'bad' was good."

Author Unknown

Part VI:
Worldview

"Perception and worldview are one's summary of life."
Asa Don Brown

"An old Cherokee chief was sharing with a grandson his philosophy of life. The elderly man told the grandson that life is like a fight between two wolves. One of the wolves was filled with envy, greed, arrogance, lies, ego, and false pride. The other wolf was filled with joy, humility, truth, compassion, and love. The grandson asked the grandfather, "Which wolf, grandfather, do you think will win the fight?" The grandfather's reply was, "The one you feed."

Author Unknown

We have been feeding the wrong wolf. Violence and the impetuous determination for higher productivity continues at any cost. Seems like many of us have forgotten the value of balance. If we are looking for balance to our worldview, where do we look for those concealed secrets, the secrets to making the world a better place?

Observing the millennials' worldview is a great place to start. My observation of their view of materialism, race relations, violence, environmental concerns are a few issues that are evolving, to a worldview of harmony, agape love and peace on earth. This evolution gives me hope for the future. For them and the generations before them, we can learn from each other; however, it all starts with me whoever you are, finding *The Real Me, The True Self.*

Identifying our traits, temperament, journaling our life story, and those penetrating questions is good food for transformation of our worldview.

Our environmental problems are only one element of the many challenges we face today. Looking back on our western history, we have lost the spirit of the Native American.

Monica and I attended a retreat based on the book *Eco-spirituality* written by Father Charles Cummings. The discussion and thoughts shared at the retreat are pertinent to the content and theme of this book, [finding the true me] As we awaken the "real me" we are building a bridge to transform our worldview.

One subject discussed at the retreat Monica and I attended was, *looking and seeing*. It was an AH-HA moment for me. The presenter asked the question of the attendees. "What is the difference between looking and seeing?" One person told of a walk by the pond outside our cabin. She described how the sun's light reflected a tree and the clouds upon the water. As she looked at the reflection of the clouds on the water, she could see an image of an angel. She was looking at the water and *seeing* an angel. Someone could have been standing beside her *looking* at water. We have to take time to see from our inner self. My AH-HA moment was seeing.

Getting in touch with your inner-self shines a light on compassion that will be infused as part of your worldview.

> *"Whether or not you find your true self depends in a large part on the moments of time we are each allotted and the choices we make in those moments, in which the deeper "I" is slowly revealed, if we are ready to see it."*
>
> Richard Rohr

This book provides one way, a template, to make known those moments, your AH-HA moments, to reach deeper and discover the real me. Depending on your temperament and traits, you may find a walk in the woods, music, poetry, reading scripture or journaling the best way to reach your deeper self.

In whatever way you find your true self, the four corridors or template in this book [the Enneagram the MBTI, your life story, journaling with the penetrating questions] will be the backbone to discernment of your journey. Discovering your strengths and weaknesses, using the tools aforementioned, are primary tools for discernment. They certainly helped me in my spiritual growth, especially when dialoguing with the penetrating questions from James Fowler's book *Stages of Faith*.

"As our perception shifts from the small picture to the total, global picture, we open ourselves to a new possibility".

Father Cummings

When shifting our perception and attitudes, we most likely will make voluntary changes to our worldview. Changes from the heart. Those changes leading to a transformed mature worldview.

To act locally and think globally!

Part VII:
Afterthoughts

"All societies, ancient or modern, primitive or sophisticated, have guided themselves by values and goals rooted in the experience of 'deep intuition'."

Willis Harman

In making my decisions and developing relationships I have learned to be sensible and realistic, based on behavior and information. However, intuition through my life has led me to many good decisions and lasting relationships in my life. My MBTI (F-feeling) *tend to base decisions primarily on values and on subjective evaluation* (T- thinking) *tend to base decisions primarily on logic and objective analysis.*

My MBTI analysis, the feeling and thinking dichotomy were a tie. The combination of the two based on experience does make sense to me.

Intuition is hard for me to put into words but best described in the dictionary as, *"direct perception of truth independent of any reasoning process."*

It is this intuition that has led me to develop lasting relationships with the contributors to this chapter of the book. I have met each of them under different circumstances, intuitively knowing that each of them would play a role in my life. I'm sure you have experienced that feeling with someone. I will forever be grateful for their contributions to this book.

After completing a draft of the book I shared it with each of them for comment and critique. Their feedback was helpful and led to several revisions. As the author I questioned, *"Are my thoughts clearly expressing the primary message?"* Are my thoughts expressed about the template going to motivate others to dig deeper to discover their true self?

I asked each person if they would be willing to share their afterthoughts reflecting of the following.

- The value you see in discovering your temperament and traits.

- Thoughts on writing your life story.

- Thoughts on the penetrating questions.

In reading their afterthoughts, hopefully you too will find added value working with the template.

Afterthoughts contributors are: Al Mirmelstein, Susan Weiss, Andy Macfarlan M.D., Tommy Hexter and Greg Pudhorodsky M.D.

- *Albert Mirmelstein*

Al and I have known each other for a number of years. We both attended Father Chester Micheal Spiritual Direction Institute (SDI). We are members of the same church. Monica and I attended a number of retreats at Our Lady of Angels Monastery in Crozet, Virginia led by Al and his wife Bev. Through these experiences Al and I know each other. Conversations and retreats with him have been a contribution to my spiritual growth.

Al's response to questions:

> *"The world will ask you who you are, and if you don't know, the world will tell you."*
>
> Carl Jung

On one level, Roger's life, experiences, and personality would appear to have little in common with mine. He grew up on a small subsistence farm in rural Nebraska. I was raised in Newport News, Virginia, a blue collar industrial city in the Virginia Tidewater. Roger's family was of German/Lutheran extraction. My father was the grandson of a Lithuanian rabbi, and my mother grew up on a farm in LA where her family attended a Pentecostal church. Roger's Meyers Briggs Type is Extraverted (E),

Sensing (S), Thinking (T), and Judging (J). Mine is Introverted (I), Intuitive (N), Feeling (F), and Perceiving (P). In terms of the Enneagram, Roger is a type 8, The Challenger. (People of this personality type are essentially unwilling to be controlled, either by others or by their circumstances; they fully intend to be masters of their fate. Eights are strong willed, decisive, practical, tough minded and energetic.) I'm a Nine, The Peacemaker (Nines are accepting, trusting, and stable. They are usually creative, optimistic, and supportive, but can also be too willing to go along with others to keep the peace. They want everything to go smoothly and be without conflict, but they can also tend to be complacent, simplifying problems and minimizing anything upsetting.)

On the other hand, I think it is fair to say that we have both been on a quest, which started roughly in mid-life, to understand the meaning of life, our place in it, and our relationship with God. That quest led us to a wise old man by the name of Msgr. Chester P. Michael and his course on spiritual direction. The upshot of that experience was a degree of fidelity to the lessons we learned there. (Perhaps most importantly, the value of a regular prayer life, and a lifelong quest for religious and spiritual education and understanding.) It was during that course that we came to understand ourselves and others on a deeper level through the Myer Briggs Type Indicator and the Enneagram. We came into contact with both ancient and modern spiritual masters, and we delved deeply into the question of why God placed us here and what God desires from our lives.

With the foregoing in mind, I will offer a brief summary of my experience with three aspects of this journey: 1) The value I see in discovering my temperament and traits; 2) My thoughts on writing my life story; and 3) My answer to one of the penetrating questions Roger addresses in this book.

The Value of Discovering My Temperament and Traits

Learning about and understanding my temperament and traits is part of a broader concept of self-discovery which began for me in my early forties with a conversion experience, baptism, Cursillo, and the Spiritual Direction Institute (SDI) course taught by Msgr. Michael. It was while taking the SDI course that I first encountered the Myers-Briggs Type Instrument (MBTI) as well as the Enneagram. (Also, and equally important to this process, was an introduction to Jungian Psychology, particularly the concepts of the Persona and the Shadow, dream work, and the Progoff Journaling method. That is a topic which goes beyond the scope of what I want to discuss in this afterward, however.)

I took the MBTI, which was a prerequisite of the course, prior to beginning SDI. Msgr. scored the instrument and gave me the results just before a Sunday mass in the summer of 1993. My type is INFP, and at the time I was working as an attorney. (Of all the 16 MBTI types, INFP may be the one most singularly ill-suited for that profession. I had never been very happy or satisfied in my career, but considered it to be a personality or character defect on my part.) Msgr. caught up with me in the narthex of the church and gave me the results, adding, "Al Mirmelstein, you are in the wrong profession!" I told him that I was well aware of that fact, but I also said that I had no idea what else I might do that would make me happy. He replied, "You should be a counselor!" These words felt like a light was shining on my soul. I went into the church, sat down, and for the first time I had a sense of the proper direction of my life.

Gradually, I formed a plan to get my counseling degree while continuing to work as an attorney, and after obtaining the degree I practiced part-time as a mental health counselor for 15 years. Although I have retired from both the attorney position and counseling, I still offer spiritual direction, which in many ways is very much related to the counseling I began after taking the MBTI many years ago.

From the foregoing, it is obvious that learning about the MBTI helped me to understand myself better and lead a more fulfilling life, but the effect it had on me went beyond that. It also helped me understand others

more clearly. As Kiersey and Bates point out in their wonderful book Please
Understand Me, *an understanding of type helps one to appreciate the value
of others with personalities very different from ours. Now I understand that
different is neither better nor worse, but rather, valuable in different ways.
As Kiersey and Bates point out, "all types are equally good." Msgr. Michael
put it in more metaphorical and spiritual terms. He said that God created
a unique and valuable human being in each one of us, and he desires us to
function like the member of an orchestra, each one making an essential,
but essentially different contribution to the whole.*

*I also learned about the Enneagram during the SDI course, but it wasn't
until more than 20 years later that I really began to appreciate the value
of this psychological tool. This is when my wife and I began to teach the
SDI course, which gave me a deeper insight into my Enneagram type (I'm a
Nine), and the impact my type has on the way I see the world.*

*I do not want to attempt a description of how the Enneagram works,
nor do I believe that this is the place to offer a detailed description of the
Nine type. Rather, I want to point out that all of the types may be described
as a sort of distorted lens through which we perceive the world and the
people in it. Importantly, we are also completely unconscious of the fact
that this lens is distorted by our own type. It is only when we realize the
dynamics of this distortion that we are able to see ourselves as we truly
are. The notion of the scales falling from one's eyes is an apt description.*

Thoughts on Writing My Life Story

*A life story can be told in two very different ways. The first would be a
factual account of what has transpired objectively. On the other hand, a
life story may be told from an interior point of view, based on psychological
and spiritual experiences. It is this latter type of life story that those of us
who took the SDI course were required to write. Msgr. Michael called it a
spiritual autobiography, and for me it came at a clear inflection point in
my life.*

As a child I can remember wanting very much to understand how people were able to believe that there was a God, when nobody, especially me, could see Him, Her, It. This was a huge conundrum for me. People talked about God, worshipped God, prayed to God, but how in the world could they be sure that there was such a thing?

I did take some consolation that there was a name for people like me – we were agnostics, which I understood to include those of us who neither believed nor disbelieved. I definitely wasn't someone who disbelieved, i.e. an atheist. To me they were just as perplexing as believers. I was simply unable to understand how either group was so utterly confident in their conclusion.

This state of perplexity lasted until I was about forty-two years old. It was at that point that I had what I later learned was a fairly typical (it seemed anything but typical at the time) "conversion experience." Actually, to name it or to try to categorize what happened seems to trivialize what was for me the most profound experience of my life – basically a direct encounter with God in the form of a vision. Actually, it would be more accurate to say that I came into contact with the "love that surpasses all understanding." Almost thirty years later I still struggle to describe the nature of this love. The best I can offer is that it is infinite, boundless, without limit, beyond my ability to even imagine in its magnitude.

Part and parcel of the vision was a clear conviction that God indeed does exist, that God wants everything that is truly important and good for us, and, in the fullness of time, we will all experience just that. Thus ended the first half of my life. Or better put, thus began the second half.

Since then, I've taken on the project of learning everything I possibly could about God and spirituality. The list of spiritual authors I've read could probably go on for several pages. Many Roger included as important to him as well. My list starts and ends with Thomas Merton, and includes Thomas Keating, Anthony deMello, Kathleen Norris, Cynthia Bourgeault, Marcus Borg, Henry Nouwen, Victor Frankl, Dorothy Day, John Sanford,

Morton Kelsey, John Cassian, Jean Shinoda Bolen, Joan Chittister, Frederick Buechner, Joseph Goldbrunner, and Christian Wyman. Carl Jung was a revelation, in the sense that he was able to reveal how the psychological and spiritual are related and support, rather than being at odds with one another. And Richard Rohr has provided a summation of almost everything I've learned from a spiritual point of view over these years.

One final note. This could be characterized as a theological point, though theology is not and never has been a very strong interest of mine. I gravitate toward the feeling side. Theology is too much in the head for my taste. However, I do believe the notion that Jesus died as a sacrifice for the expiation of our sins is wrong. Rather, I believe he did this to reveal God's infinite capacity for love and the forgiveness that accompanies it, and to show us the way to that same love and forgiveness which resides in us all.

Thoughts on a Penetrating Question

Like Roger, I believe that there is great value in considering the kinds of questions he raises and answers for himself so eloquently in his book. As Socrates said, "The unexamined life is not worth living." Still, at this stage of my life, it does seem that the answer to most of these questions, in the countless books that have been written about them, boil down to the following: God is love, and we are made in the image and likeness of that love. Therefore, our mission in life is to live a life of love according to our gifts and the light that is given to us.

Having said that, there is one nagging, essential question that actually brought me to God and which remains a mystery to me still. It is the question raised by Rabbi Harold Kushner and considered by many others — Why does God allow bad things to happen to good people? More broadly speaking, "How can a loving God permit the horrific pain and suffering that even some of the most innocent children encounter?"

There was a terrible earthquake in Mexico in the 1980's. Among the many tragic events that occurred was the collapse of an elementary school. Hundreds of children were buried and died in the rubble, not all of them immediately. Some were trapped, injured, bleeding with broken bodies for several days before dying alone in the dark.

I read about this just before I had the vision that led to my ability to believe in God, and the irony is not lost on me. How can a person believe in a loving God who would allow such a horrific thing to happen? (This is not something that can be explained with the concept of free will. Nobody's freedom led to that earthquake. It was a natural event.) The answer that came to me in my vision, which I freely admit is nonsensical, is that not only does God alleviate our suffering, but God transforms it in a way that makes it as if it never happened.

I realize that what I have just written makes no sense. There is no rational way to explain it. This leads me to a final consideration of the nature of God and the nature of human beings. For us, rational thought is the pinnacle of human understanding. But not so for God. To paraphrase God's answer to Job, "My ways are not your ways." And as Paul so beautifully put it, "Now we see through a glass darkly. Then, face to face."

•   *Susan Weiss*

It was sometime after my spiritual director Father Chester Michael died in 2014 I attended a presentation in Staunton, Va. on "Centering Prayer." After Father Michael's death I was looking for another spiritual director. The presenter for Centering Prayer was supported by Susy. This was one of those intuitive moments. At a coffee break I asked her if she would be willing to meet with me. Susy has become a great spiritual friend. Over the years our conversations have led me to write and revise this book. Her insight and support have contributed to my spiritual growth and being closer to God.

Susy's response :

Some people seem to be born seekers. People like Thomas Merton and Thomas Keating and George Fox, the founder of Quakerism. They begin asking the deep penetrating questions from an early age and probably baffle their elders. Others of us begin asking deeper questions as we learn more about life through various life experiences: we read a book that speaks to us or take a course or meet an influential person. It is said that the Buddha saw illness and old age for the first time when he left his father's home and was so moved he became an instant seeker. But I think for most of us these educational life experiences stay in the realm of the intellect—in our heads—- for a long time. We think about them. I know this is true for me.

I was always interested in what makes people tick and how people influence each other. It was natural for me to major in anthropology in college and eventually find my way to being a psychotherapist. Along the way I learned a great deal about temperaments and traits— my own and other people's. I would say my spiritual journey _was_ my psychological journey for many years. Learning who I am from a psychological point of view helped me change the direction I was looking for understanding. Instead of looking outward to other people's opinions and points of view, I began to look inward to understand who I am. There are many tools for doing this, of course......the Enneagram and the Myers Briggs are good ones.

But Roger's book suggests we go deeper, and he provides a template for doing so: writing an autobiography, gathering and sitting with quotes from writers we love and admire, and asking ourselves penetrating questions. Whew! This is hard work, Roger!

I am not a writer, but I see the value in sitting down and carefully going over my life. Looking at the highlights and the low places, gathering the memories, giving thanks for all the blessings. To me, at my stage of life, it seems a good way to prepare for death. I doubt that I have the discipline nor the temperament to actually write an autobiography, but I certainly admire people who do!

The penetrating question I chose is this: Where do you feel that you *are changing, growing, struggling or wrestling with doubt in your life at the present time? Where is your growing edge?*

I love the idea of a "growing edge"! I hope to stay on my growing edge until the day I die. At 74, I am at the stage of life where I can feel my time on earth is running out so there is more of a sense of urgency to the journey. I don't fear death and I don't really know or "care" what comes after death. But I do want to know my true self deeply and well. I have a hunch that this life is our chance to find out who we are and what our relationship is with "it all"—- which I often call God.

- ### *Andy Macfarlan M.D.*

Andy is my personal physician. I am blessed to have a trusting loving relationship with him. As my doctor, he has fortified both my physical and spiritual well being. He has been a part of my challenges of the body [physical] the pain and joy [of the heart] that is part of all our lives. In this context, Andy has shared with me the bumps along the journey. He is in a position to truly have insight to my becoming the real me.

Andy's response:

I have known Roger for over 20 years and initially got to know him well when we were paired together as mutual mentors in the Spiritual Direction Institute which has played such a prominent part in both of our lives. We share similar values, faith, temperament, and worldview, but are different enough to challenge each other on parts of all of these. He has also got a few years on me, so I look to him for how to "do retirement" well.

As Roger drew away from his successful real estate career, he filled his time and mind by both looking back and looking inward. Purposeful self review and self analysis has led to greater gratitude, generosity, satisfaction, and dependence on God (and on Monica, his saintly wife!). But the satisfaction does not fully cover the restlessness of constantly trying to learn how God connects with us and how we listen to Him. At the same time, his generosity extends his purpose in life to transparently sharing with all of us the steps he has walked in pursuing intimacy with God.

A Protestant Christian reformer started his greatest treatise with the concept that we can only really know God inasmuch as we can know ourselves. Roger's example of and suggestions for self examination in these writings are not "navel-gazing" without a goal, but ways in which he offers invitation to the riches of knowing and being known by the Creator of the Universe, the Spirit who works with us and the Savior who sets us free.

The language Roger uses is practical and you do not need to be a Christian to draw benefit from answering his questions. In fact, many of the questions and tools he mentions come from other faith traditions or have no connection to religious faith. But It is in the knowledge gained of ourselves and others that we learn to love better, the goal of life on earth. Let Roger help you find the real image of God (Image Deo) within you and you will learn many things, but especially how much you are loved. Roger is a great model of loving well!

- ***Thomas J. Hexter***

I have known Tommy for years. I used to meet with several other men and Tommy's father once a week, part of the Cursillo movement. The purpose of the meetings is simply to encourage each other to lead a Christian life. Then Tommy was a young boy and a good baseball player as I recall.

Years past and then the "Unite to Right rally" took place August 11, 2017 in Charlottesville, Va. Tommy posted his thoughts on Facebook. I was very impressed with his comments at that time [age 17] recognizing he was wise far beyond his years.

I was wondering what a millennial's response would be to

reading my script. His response to my request shows so much depth in understanding to the challenges of our world. It gives me so much hope that his generation will make our world a better place.

Tommy is now a sophomore at Grinnell College in Iowa. I am proud to say Tommy is a special friend of mine.

Tommy's response:

As long as mankind has roamed the Earth, many have pondered the true purpose of human life, both as individuals and as a species. What traits of our humanity are intrinsically valuable? In recent history, it seems as though much of our personal and collective meaning is represented by materialistic, selfish things: fancy cars, massive militaries, and powerful statures. Throughout the world and within ourselves, we feel the pull of these egotistic vices as a catalyzing force behind our actions. College is forced on young people as a means of "making social connections" and becoming educated to ensure that they will get the highest paying job. When kids flip their parents' brand-new Mercedes-Benz, the first thing that might occur to the parents is the expense of the car, not the safety of those that share our own blood. Even when we go to Church, we simply may do so to be "saved" and secure an eventual spot in Heaven. In one way or another, selfishness has shown itself in you, in me, and in all members of contemporary society.

At first glance, we probably don't see the harmful impact that these moments of selfishness have on us. After all, if we're thinking only about ourselves, doesn't that mean that we'll do what we think is best for us? When Jesus tells us that we must not be selfish but care for others, does He just not want us to be happy? No, it's actually quite the opposite: He wants us to be able to experience maximum happiness all of the time, not just when our egotistical standards are met. Our mind's thoughts and desires do not always align with God's plan for us. When all the cards are dealt, God's plan for us can only truly be experienced in our hearts.

When we live only for ourselves, we instantly become the jury, judge, and executioner for every aspect of our humanity. We begin to plan our days according to our own selfish desires. When we meet people along the way, we compare ourselves to them and try to see how we measure up. If something bad happens to us, the first thing we do is feel sorry for ourselves because it has potentially taken us off of our narrow-minded tracks. These actions only bring about anxiety, fear, and depression. Perhaps selfishness is the reason for escalating rates of mental health tragedies in our world today. If we try to make our lives perfect, we will almost certainly be let down. This is the danger of reacting to the events in our lives with only our mind's eye.

Rather, we must feel the world with our heart. Selflessness, and recognizing one's true role in relation to the grand scheme of things that God has created, can be like a rock of consistency that will always keep us above the water. Moreover, selflessness leads all of us to help one another, and everyone knows that many people helping one another is much more powerful than one person helping themselves. This is an image of the true Body of Christ.

In the year 2018, mankind seems to have almost everything it needs to thrive: high-speed internet, a global community, and massive intelligence that stems from millennia of relative failure. At this stage in humanity, WE are ready to turn the corner. The operative word in the previous sentence, as you can probably tell by the capital letters, is "WE." None of us can transform the world alone. As individual humans, we all operate with unique characteristics and goals. Once we transform ourselves, only then will the world be made perfect and unified. Alone, we are but a single grain of sand, seemingly nothing in the grand scheme of things. Together, we can make an entire beach, and create an idyllic atmosphere where none of us look to judge, but all of us live by instinct and obedience to the will of God.

My beloved Roger Mahloch's book is certainly a story of his life, but it is also something more. The tales of his trials, tribulations, and responses *lay the template for an inner dialogue with our true selves. In writing of his early life, Roger describes a sound work ethic that led him to success in the business world. He details family life including the growth of his children into beautiful and successful heirs to his family name. While these are all pieces of the puzzle that make Mr. Mahloch the devout and strong man that he is, he would surely tell you that these facts are not where his treasure lies. Rather, his treasure is in unconditional LOVE. All the time – through joy, through pain, through peace – selflessness is the response that will create the world we want to see. Roger's message contains the key to unlocking our ultimate reality. Love will create for each of us, a "Heaven on Earth."*

Now, this type of ultimate reality is certainly different for each and every human being, based on our individual traits and temperaments, as well as our upbringing and our various stages in the journey of life. In short, we all walk our own paths in this life. Some have more path behind them, some have more ahead. Others have many twists and turns. Personally, mine is only 18 years long. My road, contrary to Roger's, is pretty short, with many of the big decisions and pieces of the puzzle still undiscovered. For this reason, I look at discovering my true self as equivalent to living out my most perfect role within the Catholic and otherwise global community that I am a young member of. Where do I find myself contributing the most in the improvement of society? How can I live and evangelize the teachings of the Gospel in the world around me? Is my heart invested in contributing to the fulfillment of God's will on Earth?

Looking at the questions I just wrote, I realize they could likely be relevant to anyone on any part of their life's pathway. As we pray the words, "in the name of the Father, the Son, and the Holy Spirit, as it was in the beginning, is now, and ever shall be, a world without end, amen," we are called to understand the mystery of the trinity as an unchanging and ever-flowing stream. Within this stream, our lives may be likened to a single leaf floating down the life-giving stream of God's unceasing glory. We must recognize our own lives within the story of the universe to even begin understanding what our role in this moment of space and time might be. Therefore, it is only when we can truly understand our lives in the context of the world around us that we can unveil our selfishness and join the universal Body of Christ.

In some cases, this may be misinterpreted to think that if we want to fit in, we must be dependent on society and others to make our own judgments and actions. This will only result in becoming a reflection of society, but we are so much more. A quote from a young computer programmer named Carlo Acutis (1991-2006) says this better than I ever could: "Each of us is born an original, but we are ever in danger of dying as mere photocopies. Each of us is a unique instantiation of the love and the person of Christ. We can by the grace of the Eucharist, we can confirm and unfold that image of Christ within us or we can allow it to be reduced to a mere copy of the images provided us as substitutes. And those images come to us these days from mass education, mass entertainment, and mass politics." As I have come to age, I have realized that obsession with the objects of society is truly the way that the Devil comes into the world and tempts us to be something so much less than our true selves. Growing up, my parents taught me from a young age that service to others is the only way to find true happiness. I remember fondly one instance when I was about 5 years old, where my father, who was in Roger's Cursillo group, brought me along to a prayer session with all the members of their group to join in community to support Roger who was struggling with cancer, lifting him high with God's strength. I remember to this day thinking how brave Roger seemed to me in the face of danger. From this moment, I learned that we are all best when we open ourselves to others as a means of allowing in God's grace into the world. We can only do this when we recognize that we do not have all the power.

In my teenage years, I was often sucked in to video games, silly jokes, parties, and above all else, a sense that capitalistic individualism and consumerism might actually be the key to a happy life. As I began to age and to truly understand the evils existing in the world all around me, no longer did I believe any of these things held any real value in the world: the light and love my parents had shown me in my youth were all that I strived for. In August of 2017, a particular homily by Fr. Gregory Kandt gave my thoughts some real-world context, leading me to know individualism as a form of division, and division as the sole mechanism of the Devil – all of the vices in our world, all of the wealth, all of the patriotic nations; these are all distractions from the true context of the universe. Society has perhaps taught us to believe that we must do the best we can for ourselves because there is nothing out there that will ever unite us. However, if we take a step back from society, we recognize that all humans, past, present, and future, are all united in the fact that we are humans, that we all want to feel happiness and love, and that we are here for a reason, to be good stewards of this Earth and all of its inhabitants. We must not care for only those around us, but for those everywhere. Some traits that may be helpful for us to do so are patience, compassion, and understanding. Personally, it has been incredibly valuable for me to use these traits to realize how little I truly know in this world, and that is not such a bad thing. Naivety is a blessing – it allows us to continue learning in all cases. When we think we know everything instead of growing and learning about our true roles, our lives tend to become routinized, and we fill them with vices and meetings and friendships to try and feel some sort of comfort. Our lives are not about this kind of comfort.

Often times, we become so absorbed in the pressures of living the best possible lives (by society's standards) that the true meanings of our lives are lost. There is so much beneath the appearance of things. Instead of actively engaging our minds to truly learn about the world and bring about the global change we would like to see, we trust society to just change on its own, as if we weren't even really a part of a community of humans, all controlling each other's destinies. We all believe that *humanity can do better than it is doing right now, but to do anything about it is so infeasible that we just sit back and distract ourselves and post our views on Facebook as if the government would actually listen. To truly feel comfortable in the world, we must challenge ourselves to be opened to the comfort that lies in Christ's will for us. In order to truly live, we must die to our lazy and false selves. This is what Jesus showed the world when he died and rose again to live on the Third Day, forever at the Right Hand of God. We must give our entire lives in order to truly be free from the bounds of the divisive world that humankind has created in selfishness.*

Sometimes it can feel impossible to do so. Sometimes it seems like we'd fall behind if we gave up our selfish wants and desires. The truth is, we, all of humanity, are dead weight at this point in time. The Earth and all of its inhabitants around us are suffering as we continue to live in a society of greed and wealth with no care for what truly comes of this world. As selfishness and absorbance in only the immediate matters of our own lives becomes more prevalent, as we trust more and more that society knows what's right for us, the world becomes a place that no one seems to be able to fix. But WE, our true selves, know better. We are all called to something deeper. We are called to let go of all those things we cannot change, and to give up our lives, our worries, our wants, all for the sake of becoming the purest and most free embodiment of loving and happy humans we may be. Roger has inspired within myself, and I know within anyone reading, a deepest sense of longing to do just that. We are all humans, past, present, future, in the eyes of the world. Let us remember this, and be the light of our true selves: together, we may light up the darkness.

- *Greg Pudhorodsky M.D.*

As with the other contributors Greg and I have shared business and personal relationships for many years. It seems he shows up at times when I am exploring ways for growth at an event or conference that is not attended by most in my social and religious circles. Greg stimulates me to think outside the box.

Greg's response:

It is a well worn maxim that life is a journey, but perhaps a more useful image is to see our lives as a preparation for the universal journey we will all take. This is no small task because of unique uncertainties to this travel as we know not when we will be departing nor really what our destination is.

In light of these uncertainties, how can one approach their lives of preparation? For many the uncertainty will lead to fear. The basis of all fear is the unknown, so how much greater can the fear of the unknowable be. So great for some that it can lead to a psychic paralysis, an existential despair and inertia. At that point one can default to an outlook that life is predestined and we are pawns in a divine comedy, mirroring Macbeth - " life is a tale told by an idiot, full of sound and fury, signifying nothing".

Another alternative is a nihilistic outlook, rationalizing that if the journey is unknowable it is folly to think one can prepare for it, and rather lead a life occupied with self-indulgence in a culture of consumerism with mantras as , - he who dies with the most toys wins, - you only live once so you grab for all the gusto you can - take what you want because you deserve the best.

The third alternative and the one that Roger's book focuses on is that we use this life for the purpose it was designed, to prepare for our ultimate journey from this life to what the next holds, to prepare for the transition from time to eternity.

Do not mistake Roger's book to be a roadmap, for our itineraries do not lend themselves to a one size fits all approach. Rather he suggests a thoughtful travel guide, somewhat like the ultimate Lonely Planet.

In planning for a trip we look at travel we have done previously, what we have enjoyed, what has worked for us and what we need to avoid. It is our life history and the reflection therein, that will be a valuable asset in our planning and preparation. In preparing for a trip we need to take measure of our strengths and limitations. We certainly would ask ourself if we could climb Minchu Pichu, or bicycle for 30 miles a day to the National Parks of Utah. On this trip it is good to have insight on when are introverted in our approach versus extroverted, how do we perceive by sense or intuition and the other questions the personality indices that he suggest will tell us. And we do not prepare alone but rather in relationship and these tools will be invaluable in understanding and aiding our fellow travelers.

Lastly we need to decide what to take along. The important questions Roger presents will help us in this task. What is really necessary in our lives and what is excess baggage? What is the appropriate currency that we should exchange in this life before our travels- mindfulness, virtue, presence? What languages should we practice - prayer, meditation, centering?

Consider three travelers who will be embarking on a journey. The first is filled with anxiety and fearful of the strangeness and unfamiliarity he may encounter. This fear leads to a life of inaction and when the time to embark comes he is totally unprepared. The second traveler, in contrast of the obsessions of the first, takes a tact of denial, what the journey will bring it will bring and spends his time accumulating random trinkets and information that will prove absolutely worthless on his journey. The third traveler "prepares", using his life experiences as guide in his preparations as he knows that God writes straight by using crooked lines. He takes an honest and appreciative stock of the talents he can bring along to maneuver any terrain or climate the future will bring. He packs efficiently of the things he has in this life that will help his transition. He notes what he is missing and procures what he is lacking and discards that in life which is not useful. He is constantly diligent throughout the time before he will be departing. "But concerning that day and hour no one knows, not even the angels of heaven, nor the Son, but the Father only".

When life's final "All Aboard" comes , which traveler do you want to be? If you said Traveler #3 , you might want to pick up Roger's travel guide so you can start preparing for the most fantastic trip you will ever have in your life and the next.

Epilogue

Thank you for reading this book. For every author there is a resolve devoted to share a message with the reader. Maybe a message of diversion from the reality. Maybe one to discover or disclose, or to bring to light knowledge enriching our lives.

My resolve is to share a message, a template that assists me to grow in self-knowledge enriching my life. Increasing my faith in achieving my final goal. *Everlasting union with the Divine Reality that lives in my soul.*

Most of us have a final goal of everlasting union with the Divine Reality. When we fully live by the Golden Rule *[Do unto others as you would have them do unto you]* that is when we discover this Divine Reality is truly alive in all of us.

Using the template outlined in the book is only a few pieces of the puzzle in the search for our true self. A search that is ongoing for our entire life is to discover your soul. That is who you are. The deeper we go into discovering our temperament, traits, and dialoguing with the penetrating questions, the window to your soul is clearer. The light will shine brighter to see the true self. For those of you who journal, you may already see parallels in your entries recurring in reflection and contemplation. Parallels are revealing your true self.

Archbishop Fulton Sheen once said, *"Truth is not something that we invent. If we do, then it is a lie. Rather it is something we discover, like love."*

Father Richard Rohr's Daily Meditations consistently lead me to a deeper discovery of my true self. The following thoughts are from his meditations July 29, 2018.

> *"How we search, however, will determine what we find or even want to find. I suggest that we should be searching primarily in the universal and wise depths of recurring symbols, metaphors, and*

sacred stories, which is where humans can find deep and lasting meaning—or personal truth."

"We must never be too tied to our own metaphors as the only possible way to speak the truth. Rather, we must approach all metaphors and symbols humbly and respectfully, keeping all the inner spaces of mind, heart, and body open at the same time. I would call such respectful and non-egocentric attention "prayer."

"What do you want to let go of, and what do I want to hang on to? Instead I ask, <u>what do I want to let go of, and what do I want to give myself</u>?"

Much of our life we are trying to connect the dots. The elements of this template can help us connect the dots, *"The Who I Am."* Connecting those dots over our lifetime we gradually learn to let go of the superficiality of our rational mind, much of what we try to control. Little by little, parts of us die to knowing there always will be the unknowing. *The seeds of faith and humility is knowing part of life is not knowing.* You can't think your way to God. Love, not your intellect, grows the God space within you. Knowledge and information is not transformation. Getting to know your real self can lead to something lasting and transcendent.

There are other ways and templates that will help us connect those dots. Templates and commitments that will enhance our quest to discover the real me. The following are several thoughts and disciplines shared with me by Msgr. Chester Michael, my spiritual director.

1. The first is about balance. **The Three P's, Power, Pleasure and Possessions** — When our focus is excessive on any one of the three, we have shut our eyes to growth. All three are good, but only when they are in balance. Discovering your true self will expose areas where we are out of balance. Balance between knowing and not knowing.

2. **Give one hour a day, one day a month, and one week a year to God**—This is a commitment to allocate time to discovering the divine reality within you. Each breath we take from this moment to the instant of our death when your breath stops, is the time allotted to each of us. The choice is, how do you want to use it?

3. **The Three R'S— Read, Reflect, Rest.** Reading is the arsenal to knowledge. Reflection is absorption of words read. In reflection I find writing a one page summary [one page book report] is an excellent aid in my reflection and contemplation in search of my true self.

4. **Create Your Mission Statement** — I'M WORKING ON MINE

AFFIRMATIONS

I GIVE ONE HOUR A DAY, ONE DAY A MONTH,
ONE WEEK A YEAR TO GOD

I WILL WATCH MY TONGUE

ALWAYS BE POSITIVE WITH OTHER PEOPLE

STAY CALM AND COLLECTED NO MATTER WHAT

EXPECT THE BEST TODAY

STAY CONSCIOUS OF MY NEED TO EXERCISE

EAT LESS AND HEALTHY

MISSION STATEMENT

TO DISCOVER AND ACCEPT WHO I AM AND SHIFT FROM
MATERIAL TO SPIRITUAL VALUES.

TO GROW IN MY RELATIONSHIP WITH GOD AND LEARN TO
ENJOY THE PRESENT MOMENT.

TO ADAPT A MORE SIMPLE LIFE STYLE AND TO FIND MY
REAL PURPOSE IN LIFE.

"When all your desires are distilled; You will cast just two votes; to love more, And be happy."

Hafez

Discovering and becoming your true self leads to more love and happiness.

Made in the USA
Middletown, DE
02 July 2019